PS
374
.N4
W367
1993

Warren, Kenneth W.
  (Kenneth Wayne)

Black and white
  strangers.

$27.50

DATE			

JAN   1994

BLACK AND WHITE
STRANGERS

**BLACK LITERATURE
AND CULTURE**
*A series edited
by Houston A. Baker, Jr.*

KENNETH W. WARREN

BLACK AND WHITE
STRANGERS

Race and American Literary Realism

THE UNIVERSITY OF CHICAGO PRESS
Chicago & London

Kenneth W. Warren is associate professor in the
Department of English, University of Chicago.

THE UNIVERSITY OF CHICAGO PRESS, CHICAGO 60637
THE UNIVERSITY OF CHICAGO PRESS, LTD., LONDON
© 1993 BY THE UNIVERSITY OF CHICAGO
All rights reserved. Published 1993
Printed in the United States of America
02 01 00 99 98 97 96 95 94 93   1 2 3 4 5
ISBN: 0-226-87384-6 (cloth)

Library of Congress Cataloging-in-Publication Data

Warren, Kenneth W. (Kenneth Wayne)
    Black and white strangers: race and American literary realism/
Kenneth W. Warren.
        p.   cm.—(Black literature and culture)
    Includes bibliographical references and index.
        1. American fiction—19th century—History and criticism. 2. Afro-
Americans in literature.   3. American fiction—20th century—
History and criticism.   4. James, Henry, 1843–1916—Political and
social views.   5. Literature and society—United States—History.
6. Race relations in literature.   7. Realism in literature.
8. Whites in literature.   I. Title.   II. Series.
PS374.N4W367   1993
810.9'3520396073—dc20   92-42646
                                                               CIP

∞ *The paper used in this publication meets the minimum requirements of the*
American National Standard for Information Sciences—Permanence of Paper
for Printed Library Materials, ANSI Z39.48-1984.

LITERATURE AND LANGUAGE

To Mom and Dad

CONTENTS

Contents

ACKNOWLEDGMENTS

This project began as a dissertation under the direction of Jay Fliegelman, whose advice and encouragement during a time of great uncertainty were invaluable to me. Since then, the contributions of friends and colleagues have kept me moving in the right direction. Thomas Lutz, Albert Gelpi, George Fredrickson, and Arnold Rampersad helped me clarify my ideas during the early stages of writing. As the book neared completion, Carl Smith, Gerald Graff, William Veeder, and James Chandler took time to read the manuscript in its entirety, making helpful suggestions and last-minute criticisms.

I owe a debt of gratitude to Northwestern University for a President's Fund in the Humanities fellowship which provided me with a year's leave at a crucial stage of the project. I am also indebted to Alan Thomas, my editor at the University of Chicago Press, and to Houston Baker, the editor of the series in which this work appears. I would be remiss if I failed to mention the Press's outside readers, whose critiques of my manuscript were both challenging and supportive, and David Schabes, whose copyediting was marvelous.

In the end, though, nothing would have been possible without the support, understanding, and love of the people who have lived with me and this book for what seems like a lifetime. My children, Lenora, Mercedes, Marcus, and Gregory have been wonderful throughout the process. If this book were half as good as they have been it would be a masterpiece. Above all else and all others, however, my wife, Maria, as critic and companion, deserves more thanks than I can possibly put into words.

INTRODUCTION

The "realists" profess to be truth-tellers, but are the worst of
falsifiers, since they tell only the weakest and meanest part of
the grand truth which makes up the continued story of every
life.

Albion Tourgée
"The South as a Field for Fiction"

From Abraham Lincoln's greeting to Harriet Beecher Stowe—"So
this is the little lady who made this big war"[1]—to Mark Twain's
"wild proposition" that "Sir Walter [Scott] had so large a hand in
making Southern character before the war, that he is in great
measure responsible for the war,"[2] assessments of the literature
written and read by Americans from the mid- to the late nineteenth century have offered competing accounts of how narrative
fictions shaped American society of that period. Though not always uttered with Lincoln's or Twain's wit and aplomb, arguments
about fiction's responsibility for or opposition to the social order
that took shape during the post–Civil War years have proved un-
derstandably irresistible. The rise of American literary realism in
the late nineteenth century was accompanied by, and perhaps fu-
eled by, broad claims about the social consequences of reading fiction. Twain's censure of Scott suggests, for example, that the reconstruction of the South following the Civil War entailed a
reconstruction of its literary habits, a proposition perhaps not as
"wild" as Twain believed, judging from the number of other Americans who held similar beliefs. A novelist and progressive Southerner, George Washington Cable not only endorsed but seemed to
embody Twain's notions. Praised by the author of *Huckleberry Finn*
as a Southerner who "did not write in the southern style,"[3] Cable

explicitly linked literary reform with the political reconstruction of the South, declaring in an essay titled "My Politics" that he "longed to see the emancipation of literature in the South. It is not yet complete."[4]

Of course, one consequence of connecting literary styles and social change is that social criticism becomes implicitly, and often explicitly, literary criticism, leaving fiction itself vulnerable to questions about its complicity in maintaining the very order it seeks to challenge. The list of conditions that prevent or subvert change can then include novels and the various strategies of representation that they employ. Not only is it possible to hold up historical "facts" such as economic panics and demographic shifts in order to say, "Here are reasons why the social order failed to respond to, or rebuffed, the critique being offered," but the critic can point to a novel's textual strategies and assert, "Here is what the novel itself did to subvert or contain its own critique."

Their persuasiveness notwithstanding, claims about the social effects of literature have always proved tenuous and subject to revision. It was long held that American realism's failures, both political and aesthetic, resulted from the stranglehold of sentimental and romantic forms on the American imagination. Shared by Twain, Cable, William Dean Howells, and later generations of American literary scholars, this position was clearly articulated in the mid-1960s by works like Larzer Ziff's *The American 1890s: Life and Times of a Lost Generation,* which chronicled the shortcomings of American realists at the end of the last century. Allowing "belief to control experience,"[5] turn-of-the-century writers failed to confront directly the disturbing realities of an industrialized and urbanized American scene.

By contrast, recent critical works often claim that realistic principles themselves, and not some romantic atavisms, account for the realistic novel's evasiveness and ineffectiveness as a political gesture. More specifically, Leo Bersani has argued that "the critical judgments passed on society in nineteenth-century fiction are qualified by a form which provides this society with a reassuring myth about itself. The realistic novel gives us an image of social fragmentation contained within the order of significant form— and it thereby suggests that the chaotic fragments are somehow socially viable and morally redeemable."[6]

Bersani's analysis rests on the claim that the realistic novelist's commitment to psychologically coherent characters, coupled with an ability to marshal a myriad of details into a significant form, implicated realism in nineteenth-century society's inability to tolerate, and unwillingness to investigate, the alternative social possibilities that disorder might contain. "A reassuring belief in psychological unity and intelligibility . . . blinds both the novelist and his society to the psychic discontinuities and incoherence from which all our fragmented experience ultimately derives. A myth about psychic order and structure helps to contain, and to limit, all critiques of disorder. It also makes it practically impossible to begin experimenting with nondestructive versions of fragmented desires."[7]

Bersani's criticisms are at once more precise and more vague than Twain's censures of Southern literature—more precise because they supplement an account of what happens in realistic novels with a discussion of how the novels work to make meanings; more vague in that their scope is so vast. The realistic novel, if one pushes the implications of Bersani's argument, could be made complicit with everything in European and American societies of the nineteenth century except, it seems, the forms of disorder that might have provided individuals with less destructive modes of behavior. At this extreme, studies like Bersani's appear vulnerable to Gerald Graff's charge that they are "prone to facile analogies which conflate rhetorical and political terms."[8] This vulnerability, however, does not dissolve the usefulness of such works but serves as a warning that one must take care in making and defending one's claims.

For such studies are useful in posing questions about literature and society during the Gilded Age that might make possible the telling of a story about that period somewhat different from, but at least as compelling as, those previously told. If realism in its general outlines contributed to society's intolerance of psychic and social disorder and difference, can that claim be refined to examine the role of realism during a more narrowly circumscribed period and in relation to more precisely defined social phenomena?[9] More specifically, the story of African Americans from emancipation through the turn of the century is a story of social intolerance and violent suppression of difference and perceived disorder. Is there a way to locate the realistic novel in that story without assuming realism's general complicity with, or inherent opposition to,

either the initial efforts to make freedom real for American freedmen or the nation's acquiescence to the white "Redemption" of
the South and ultimately to the "separate but equal" decision
handed down by the U.S. Supreme Court in 1896?

The connection of realism to race is not made idly. Like many of
their American studies counterparts, students of African-American
literature have often assumed the necessary connection between
an acceptance of realistic methods and social progress in the realm
of race. Sterling Brown, in *The Negro in American Fiction,* and Alain
Locke, in essays such as "The Saving Grace of Realism," hailed realistic characterization and plot as a necessary adjunct to the acceptance of black Americans as full participants in American society.[10] In fact, one might argue that the revisionist critique of the
Dunning School's Reconstruction historiography was realistic in
nature. The Dunning School, named after historian William A.
Dunning, helped crystalize a view of Radical Reconstruction as a
misguided experiment in racial equality that led only to corruption. This view reigned until revisionist historians, including most
prominently W. E. B. Du Bois, argued that Dunning and his follow-
ers, like failed realists, had allowed their beliefs to control their experience, sacrificing "scholarly objectivity on the altar of racial
bias."[11]

However, despite the faith placed in realism by scholars like
Locke and Brown during the 1930s and 1940s, and the critical
force that realistic logic evidenced in the historical scholarship of
1940s and 1950s, the role of realism in African-American letters of
the postbellum period has been treated with ambivalence, suspicion, and outright hostility. Robert Bone's still-important study of
the African-American novel found early realism to be a minor
force for most turn-of-the-century black writers. These authors
were "not influenced by the incipient social realism of Howells and
Garland; or by the regionalism of Harte, Twain, and Sarah Orne
Jewett, or by the naturalism of Dreiser and Norris; and certainly
not by the stylistic subtlety and urbane cosmopolitanism of
James."[12] But long before Bone had largely dismissed the effects of
realism on early African-American writers, a contemporary of
Howells and James had offered a more searing commentary on realism and race. In the 1880s Albion Tourgée—novelist, Reconstruction jurist, and counsel for the plaintiff in *Plessy* v. *Ferguson*—
declared that realism was inadequate to the task of conveying "the

grand truth which makes up the continued story of every life."[13] Having predicted in the 1860s that "Southern life would furnish to the future American novelist his richest and most striking material,"[14] Tourgée elaborated his argument in 1888 by saying that in order to represent the social changes experienced by African Americans since the Civil War, writers would have to embrace romanticism: "The life of the Negro as a slave, freedman, and racial outcast offers undoubtedly the richest mine of romantic material that has opened to the English-speaking novelist since the Wizard of the North discovered and depicted the common life of Scotland."[15] Directly contradicting Twain, Tourgée deemed the fictional style of Sir Walter Scott the only means of rendering truthfully the "reality" of the South.

Among Tourgée's evidence that realism was inadequate to the task of representing "the African" was the low profile kept by Henry James and William Dean Howells in the flood of stories about Southerners: "Hardly a novelist of prominence, except Mr. Howells and Mr. James, but has found it necessary to yield to the prevailing demand and identify himself with Southern types. Southern life does not lend itself readily to the methods of the former. It is earnest, intense, full of action, and careless to a remarkable degree of the trivialities which both these authors esteem the most important features of real life."[16] In making his criticism of Howells and James, however, Tourgée overlooked James's characterization of a Mississippian, Basil Ransom, in *The Bostonians* (1886), and was prematurely counting Howells out of the picture, for in the 1890s Howells would write a "race" novel, *An Imperative Duty*, and would depict a Southerner, Colonel Woodburn, in *A Hazard of New Fortunes*. But James's own admission that his fictional Southern hero "remains a rather vague & artificial creation,"[17] along with a general critical dissatisfaction with Howells's *An Imperative Duty* and the rather minor role played by Woodburn in *A Hazard*, might be viewed as support for Tourgée's claim that romance was the generic vehicle for truth in the representation of race and the South.

But for its focus on the gothic, Leslie Fiedler's *Love and Death in the American Novel* (1960) echoes in many respects the critique of realism that Tourgée had articulated almost seventy years earlier. "Only the American tradition of symbolic gothicism," Fiedler intones, "which from Poe and Melville to Twain and Faulkner has never ceased to confront the problem of the Negro, has proved in an age of realism adequate to the complexities of life in the American South."[18] Fiedler then goes on to claim that "to discuss, for instance, in the light of pure reason the Negro problem in the United States is to falsify its essential mystery and unreality; it is a gothic horror of our daily lives. If Ralph Ellison's *Invisible Man* seems, as a novel written by a Negro about the Negro's plight, superior to any of the passionate, incoherent books of Richard Wright, this is because Ellison has bypassed all formulas of protest and self-pity and *cast off the restrictions of mere realism*."[19] Realism, which was figured by Howells as a means "to widen the bounds of sympathy, to level every barrier against aesthetic freedom, to escape from the paralysis of tradition,"[20] is refigured by Fiedler, within the realm of race, as restrictive and formulaic. Realism can only evade or falsify the true nature of black "reality" and American racism. As further evidence of realism's failure to grasp fully the complexities of race in America, one can point to the vexed relationship that Howells maintained with Paul Laurence Dunbar and Charles Chesnutt. Though a strong supporter of both writers, Howells could not escape racial condescension in his attitude toward their work. His visions of realism could accept fully neither Dunbar's efforts to expand his voice beyond dialect verse nor Chesnutt's attempt to make the novel face the grim racial situation at the turn of the century.[21]

More recently, censures of realism by vernacular or blues critics of African-American literature suggest not only that realism has failed to provide a successful representation of African-American experience but also that the black literary tradition has been in some sense deformed or "stunted" by a rigid adherence to realism. Henry Louis Gates, Jr., has argued that black writers themselves have been misled by the ideological assumptions of social realism and too often "have conceived their task to be the creation of an art that reports and directly reflects brute, irreducible, and ineffable 'black reality,' a reality that in fact was often merely the formulaic fictions spawned by social scientists whose work intended to reveal a black America dehumanized by slavery, segregation, and racial discrimination, in a one-to-one relationship of art to life".[22] And in phrasing reminiscent of Fiedler's claims about Ralph Ellison, Gates has asserted that the success of Toni Morrison's *Beloved* derives from its author's having slipped the bonds of realistic narrative strategies. He maintains that "only by stepping outside of the limitations of realism and entering a realm of myth could Morrison, a century after its abolition, give a voice to the silence of enslavement."[23]

Gates's praise of Morrison's recourse to myth underscores a key point. Many of realism's detractors accept the logic of linking literary genres with specific social, political, and intellectual outcomes. Whether the alternative form is "myth," "gothic," or "romance," disparagers of realism have suggested that an orientation toward other genres might yield better literary criticism, better novels, or even a better society. Indeed, a better criticism and better fiction seem so much to imply social change that Gates, who often derides tendencies to collapse political and literary concerns in a "one-to-one" relationship, nonetheless feels that a new critical orientation is necessary if African-American critics are "to assume our own propositions, and to stand within the academy as politically responsible and responsive parts of a social and cultural African-American whole." For Gates an attention to the "literary" qualities of a black canon is necessary if we are not to "remain indentured servants to white masters, female and male, and to the Western tradition."[24] Our emancipation—textual, institutional, and psychic—will ensue from our various literary choices.

Certainly there are theorists who question the capacity of any literary form to sustain an oppositional politics, especially within the domain of consumer capitalism. "The only relation literature as such has to culture as such is that it is part of it," in the words of Walter Benn Michaels.[25] I invoke this position not in the way of endorsement but because its formulation exerts considerable pressure on the arguments at play here, arguments which stress the significance of generic differences in staking out political territory. In a very literal sense Michaels's dismissal of the oppositional status of literary genres is borne out in the biographies of Tourgée and Howells, who differed on the question of genre but whose historical role in the battle against racism was roughly compatible. That is, to the extent that one describes the politics of Tourgée and Howells as oppositional, the correspondence of realism to that politics is uncertain.

For his part, Tourgée was quite frank in questioning the link be-

tween effective literary representation and any politics of racial uplift. Asserting that "our literature has become not only Southern in
type, but distinctly Confederate in sympathy," Tourgée explained
that "sentiment does not always follow the lead of conviction, and
romantic sympathy is scarcely at all dependent upon merit."[26] Neither the capacity of literature to elicit sympathy from its readers
nor the ability of various social groups to capture the imagination
of society at large derives from the rightness or wrongness of the
cause espoused. Tourgée's endorsement of a romanticism that was
Confederate in sympathy was not an endorsement of Confederate
sympathies. His activities as a federal judge during Congressional
Reconstruction and his role as counsel for the plaintiff in *Plessy* v.
Ferguson located him politically with the realist Howells who championed the cause of black writers and was a charter member of the
NAACP. The divergent literary tastes of these men did not point to
opposing political beliefs.

But even in face of contradictory political appropriations which
might undercut claims of inherent genre politics, the question of
literary complicity is not evaded. Many such claims rest upon a sub-
tle presentation of the novel's articulation within structures of
power. Reading Henry James through the lens of Michel Foucault,
Mark Seltzer has argued that Western society operates by a "*cou-
pling* of power and resistance. Not merely tolerating but requiring
resistances, not merely controlling and classifying but also creating
and producing the abnormalities, anomalies, and delinquencies
that extend the range of its operations."[27] The resistance to power
that seems available within literature is the very means by which
power in the novel is exercised. Despite their differences, Seltzer's
Foucauldian reading agrees very well with Bersani's evaluation of
realism in stressing the limits imposed on realistic political critique. The realistic novel creates the discrepancies and discords
which it then encompasses in a larger, coherent form.

But linking too hastily resistance and the extension of power can
obscure the nuances of the historical and cultural work that fictions perform. If one looks at a novel like Mark Twain's *Huckleberry
Finn* (which Bersani does briefly)[28] the factors undermining its critique of American racism may be related to the novel's endorsement of a coherent self but cannot be fully explained by that endorsement. As compelling as Bersani's characterizations of
realistic novels are, they seem to be "true of the American novel of

the period only to a limited extent."[29] Many late nineteenth-century American narratives do challenge the idea of psychological coherence (in Twain's corpus *Pudd'nhead Wilson* comes most readily to mind) but nonetheless seem to operate ambiguously in regard to racism. It is not only that Bersani's description of what counts as oppositional overlooks the possibility that "the capitalism of the late nineteenth and early twentieth centuries acted more to subvert the ideology of the autonomous self than to enforce it."[30] His argument likewise does not attend sufficiently to the possibility that nineteenth-century challenges to repressive orders failed not only because of their internal flaws but also because these challenges were countered by historical actors who believed their interests to be imperilled by changes to the status quo.

It may be, then, that one must try to account for the strong belief in the emancipatory powers of realism by looking at the effects of those beliefs within and without literary texts. That is, one must complement the vision of realism as a literary-political gesture inherently subverted by its mode of being with a vision of realism as a gesture that was also subverted within historical time. Certainly, a great many recent accounts of American literary realism have either heeded or questioned the call to "historicize" American literature.[31] And these works, by such scholars as June Howard, Amy Kaplan, Carolyn Porter, Eric Sundquist, Bersani, Michaels, and Seltzer have influenced and challenged my thinking considerably.[32] Yet by linking the stories of black America from emancipation through the "nadir" of the 1890s with the story of American realism during the period "in which American writers felt most compelled, and tried hardest, to become 'realists'—and failed,"[34] I hope to add to this discussion of realism in particular and to the discussion of American literature in general an investigation of the mutually constitutive construction of "black" and "white" texts in American literature.

The racially heterogeneous makeup of American society, coupled with white America's anxiety about its own identity within an international context, have made central a dynamic of racial revision within American literature. As Ralph Ellison describes the workings of this relationship,

> the white American has charged the Negro American with being without past or tradition (something which strikes the

white man with a nameless horror), just as he himself has
been so charged by European and American critics with a
nostalgia for the stability once typical of European cultures;
and the Negro knows that both were "mammy-made" right
here at home. What's more, each secretly believes that he
alone knows what is valid in the American experience, and
that the other knows he knows but will not admit it, and each
suspects the other of being at bottom a phony.[34]

Staring at one another across the void of American identity, African and European Americans have been constructing themselves
and each other, each side trying to lay claim to an unchallenged
cultural legacy and each failing (to paraphrase Twain) to prove un-
ambiguous title. As each side strives to construct a *sui generis* account of its own heritage, the Other insists upon emerging in unexpected and embarrassing places.

The troubling emergence of traces of other traditions within pu-
tatively pure literary historical accounts potentially undercuts attempts to locate what one scholar has termed "the culturally specific in Afro-American life and expression."[35] While it remains
important, intellectually and politically, to address the multiple
factors that have set African Americans apart from their fellow citizens, it is equally worthwhile to attend to the pressures that challenge cultural distinctiveness. The point is not to construct a racially integrated literary utopia but to highlight the intellectual
and cultural anxieties that have made separatism and discrimination in a variety of forms seem viable solutions to the social problems of a supposedly democratic society.

By dramatizing the anxieties that were contemporary with the
rise of realism in American society—a society which after a less than
halfhearted pursuit of racial democracy sought to fix itself coherently according to racial criteria—I hope to reveal that concerns
about "race" may structure our American texts, even when those
texts are not "about" race in any substantive way. In a multiracial,
multiethnic society, race, particularly black/white racial difference, emerges not merely as a problem but as part of the discursive
building blocks that make expression—political and aesthetic—
possible. Consequently, it seems timely to heed Toni Morrison's
call for an "examination and re-interpretation of the American
canon, the founding nineteenth-century works, for the 'unspeak-

able things unspoken'; for the ways in which the presence of Afro-Americans has shaped the choices, the language, the structure—the meaning of so much American literature. A search, in other words, for the ghost in the machine."[36]

In a similar vein, William Boelhower has recently suggested that "the ethnic self . . . may choose either to develop a local cultural map or float about in the dominant culture as exegete or interpreter of the ethnic traces inscribed everywhere (but nowhere) in the American topology."[37] This project might be seen as fleshing out those traces or ghosts.

My enterprise, of course, raises some crucial questions about methods, questions which I feel cannot be answered all at once. The risks of such an undertaking are, perhaps, obvious. To describe race as being always at work is potentially to totalize it in the way that Bersani totalizes psychological coherence. If race is everywhere, then any question we might ask is presumably already answered, and rather than arguing that the realistic novel's commitment to psychologically coherent characters acted to contain its social critique, we will find ourselves similarly theorizing that the freedom from tradition sought by realists was limited by the inability of these writers to get beyond the racist assumptions held by many Americans of the late nineteenth century. Admittedly, I think that such a contention is in large part true. I also think, however, that the story is more complicated than that, and more importantly, that the critical concerns of realists intersected in sometimes unexpected and unintentional ways with the politics of race.

A second danger is the seductiveness of analogies and the "false cognates" they offer. Critics have long noted the prominence of metaphors of enslavement in realist novels, especially in the works of Henry James. "James's novels," writes Daniel Schneider "explore enslavement as systematically as Dante explores hell."[38] And yet despite this acknowledgment, Schneider's study proceeds as if James's metaphors of enslavement bear no relation to the upheavels caused by the Civil War and Reconstruction. In the years following emancipation, the word "slavery" was used to describe everything from the domestic condition of women to the practice of pirating works published by foreign authors. "Black slavery, though abolished by the Thirteenth Amendment, retained a key place in American racial thought from Reconstruction to World War I," John David Smith has argued. "Many influential writers . . . identified black slavery with the broad racial and economic issues of their own day. For them slavery served as a crucial metaphor, a comparative model for what they perceived as new forms of servitude."[39] Though Smith's claims seem unarguable, and though arguments which divorce questions of enslavement from the social realities of James's era need to be challenged, the degree to which the "racial" elements of slavery were evoked by various writers can never be assumed. Used simply as a synonym for tyranny, slavery might not always carry with it the full social and historical weight of African-American enslavement.

The same can be said for other key terms. Quite provocatively, the same year that Du Bois published *The Souls of Black Folk,* which commented on the black American's "double-consciousness," Henry James's *The Ambassadors* chronicled the psychological odyssey of its hero, Lambert Strether, who "was burdened . . . with the oddity of a *double consciousness.*"[40] As tempting as it might be to read into Strether's divided aims an awareness of Du Bois (the essay in which Du Bois first employed the term was published in August 1897 in the *Atlantic Monthly* before James began writing the novel in earnest) the temptation must be resisted. Most likely, Du Bois and James adapted the term from a host of other sources.[41] A firmer link between the two authors is James's mention of *The Souls of Black Folk* in *The American Scene.* And it is such concretions, and not the teasing repetition of Du Bois's key term, that will guide my analyses.

In the pages that follow, then, I will read some of the fictional and critical works of Henry James in order to demonstrate that racial concerns shaped James's aesthetic even when his texts were not specifically "about" race in any substantive way. This reading of James is not meant to be comprehensive but suggestive, an indication of the possibilities that an attention to race may hold for further studies of American literature. It should be said here that realism, as a generic term, is a noisy and roomy compartment often expanded to include an annex for naturalists and impressionists. In this compartment one can expect to encounter such disparate figures as William Dean Howells, Henry James, Kate Chopin, Edith Wharton, Charles Chesnutt, Mark Twain, Stephen Crane, Theodore Dreiser, Frank Norris, and Sinclair Lewis. By giving center stage to Henry James and William Dean Howells in the present study, I do not mean to ignore the various controversies surrounding this generic term. Given, however, that African-American liberation during this period was often figured as a desire to enter a preexisting social order, it seems useful to highlight a certain aspect of the realism of the 1880s, which though not exclusive to this period, certainly loomed larger for these writers than perhaps for others. The works of James and Howells, for example, tend to entertain a belief that society or properly functioning social institutions possess the potential to shape or reform the individual. In these novels, where a person comes from, what a person does, and how that person was raised truly matter.

By contrast in the writings of Dreiser and Norris where brute forces rule, social institutions such as family and profession seem merely to glance off the individuals they touch, hardly changing their trajectories and failing to impress upon them habits and beliefs with which to negotiate their worlds. The broken or incomplete families in the fictions of James and Howells generally provide an opening through which society can be seen working, not always benevolently, but at least as something that works, as something that can be threatened, and as something that can be strengthened or changed. The broken or dysfunctional families in Crane's *Maggie* or Dreiser's *Sister Carrie* point to a social order that has been blasted by forces it has yet to figure out how to control.

The realistic novel's focus on the importance and fragility of the social order proved crucial during these decades. As my reading of James takes shape, I will argue that James's work, and that of the realists in general, assisted in the creation of a climate of opinion that undermined the North's capacity to resist Southern arguments against political equality for African Americans during the 1880s and 1890s through its conflicted participation in discussions about the American social order. On the one hand, works like Howells's *The Rise of Silas Lapham* mythologized the alliance of culturally conservative elites and new capitalists, thus resisting the "radical democratic ideology" that underwrote Radical Reconstruction.[42] On the other hand, these fictions often evinced a commitment to imagining the consequences that would ensue from an "extension of the field of democratic struggles to the whole of civil society and the state."[43] This latter aspect of realism has been slighted in recent studies but is crucial for understanding the place of realism in late nineteenth-century debates on race. The insistence of writers like Henry James on seeing the political in terms of its social manifestations made patently clear the scale of social disruptions that would be necessary to accommodate democratic change.

In part for this reason, my assessment of James's works extends well beyond my first chapter; his writings, in fact, function somewhat as a leitmotif. The attentiveness to the social realm in James's fictional and critical texts, along with his propensity for exploring human ambiguities seemed an apt lens through which to view this period. An equally important reason for James's prominence here, however, is that in reexamining an aspect of what R. W. B. Lewis terms the James "family's settled reputation for being entirely divorced from the great public crises and the burning public issues of its era,"[44] I hoped to address some of our contemporary concerns about the relation of aesthetics to politics and to do so in a way that did not simply collapse one term onto the other.

In the chapter following my reading of James I highlight the links that were commonly being made between the reconstruction of the Union—a process that continued long after Federal Reconstruction had come to an end—and the role that fiction was to play in that process. Glancing briefly at some discussions of literature and the Reconstruction effort in the first issue of *The Nation,* I then treat more specifically the *Century* magazine from the early 1880s. During these years the *Century,* edited by Richard Watson Gilder, took up the question of sectional reconciliation, publishing exchanges between George Washington Cable, who tried to mark out a moderate position in favor of civil equality, and his Southern critics, who accused him of advocating social equality. The magazine also serialized fiction by William Dean Howells, Henry James, and Mark Twain. Within these novels and political discussions one can locate the uneasy and eventually unsatisfactory accommodations of literary and political radicalism with more moderate positions. At a time when Cable, the preeminent white liberal spokesman on race relations, was arguing that civil rights could be granted to blacks with a minimal disruption of prevailing genteel mores, realism was calling into question the traditions, habits, and customs that race liberals pointed to as natural brakes on the engines of social change. As the civil rights movement of the 1960s has proved, such a calling into question was a necessary component of real challenges to American racism. In the 1880s, however, the implications of realism's political critique outstripped the capacity of editors, society, and realists themselves to absorb the full political import of their literary practices.

The third chapter focuses more tightly on realism's critique of sentimentalism, specifically its argument with Harriet Beecher Stowe's *Uncle Tom's Cabin*. Although for a writer like Howells, technique and not politics was the central problem with Stowe's landmark text, disentangling a criticism of its aesthetics from a criticism of its politics became progressively difficult. The first part of the chapter illustrates how the efforts by realists to distinguish realistic characterization from sentimental delineations of character also helped, paradoxically, to define social distinctions between the majority of black and white Americans as "real" and ineffaceable.

The second part of the chapter, by focusing centrally on the relationship between James's *The Bostonians* and Stowe's *Uncle Tom's Cabin*, argues that the definitional elasticity of the term *sentimental* helped legitimate Southern critiques of Northern progressive political traditions. Inasmuch as critical and fictional "revisions" of Stowe's masterwork can be seen as linking Northern realists, like James and John William De Forest with racist, radical Southerners like Thomas Dixon, author of *The Leopard's Spots* (1902) and *The Clansman* (1905), what emerges is an inadvertent alliance between Northern realism and Southern romance in an assault on the political idealism of the New England tradition.

The fourth chapter juxtaposes James's *The American Scene* (1907), Frances E. W. Harper's *Iola Leroy* (1892), and W. E. B. Du Bois's *The Souls of Black Folk* (1903), all of which share deep misgivings about the triumph of Gilded Age values. What this juxtaposition illustrates, however, is the complex and often contradictory ways that notions of racial identity could figure in literary critiques of America's commercial order. While tracking the social, aesthetic, and moral costs of racism and consumer capitalism, these works could nonetheless articulate differently the values of black and white identities.

My concluding chapter is a discussion of contemporary African-American literary criticism and theory. To describe this book as African-Americanist—a book which scants the work of black realist Charles W. Chesnutt, devotes considerable attention to only two black writers (Harper and Du Bois) and even more attention to works by white authors, many of which do not directly take up matters of race—demands some explanation. In fact, an observation made by Elaine Showalter about a different work seems to apply here: "The reader of the volume must wonder whether the installation of 'race' will displace the study of black literature, and reinstitute a familiar canon, now seen from the perspective of the racial trope."[45] As a scholar and critic of both "black" literature and "mainstream" American literature, I feel called upon to take such a charge seriously.

Hazel Carby has recently written that "work that uses race as a central category does not necessarily need to be about black women."[46] Accepting Carby's formulation I would like to extend and emend it by saying that works for which race can serve as a useful tool of inquiry and works that can reveal to us the way that race has shaped and is shaping our history need not be about race. What I argue here is that despite its contributions to literary study, canon-based criticism of African-American literature has entailed a variety of liabilities, from recapitulating in black vernacular the assumptions of American ahistoricism to taking for granted apolitical notions of black unity that impoverish our understanding of our intellectual and political history.

I am not the first to make these arguments. Theodore O. Mason, Jr., has suggested that "canon-formation as an enterprise be junked, in favor of more persistent textual and cultural analysis."[47] And others, including Kwame Anthony Appiah, Hazel Carby, Adolph Reed, Jr., and Werner Sollors, have in various ways pointed out the limitations imposed by a canon-based critique on efforts to investigate the myriad roles that the idea of race has played in creating and deforming imaginative literature written in America and indeed in shaping and deforming the whole of America.[48] Additionally, Aldon Lynn Nielsen has examined the maintenance of and cultural work performed by "white discourse" in canonical American poets of the twentieth century.[49] What makes necessary a further refinement and articulation of these arguments is the persistence of charges that to problematize claims about black particularity is to play into the hands of white hegemony.[50] Such charges come in a variety of forms, ranging from attacks on those who use post-structuralist theories to attacks on those who eschew academic theory. Against such apparently contradictory ways of inflecting challenges to and defenses of the black "difference" it seems imperative to point up again the assumptions behind these arguments and, ultimately, to place them within the context of our expectations about the political effects of our critical practices.

ONE

Reading Henry James

In heaven there'll be no algebra
No learning dates or names
But only playing golden harps
And reading Henry James
   —Robert Louis Stevenson

I

THE ETHEREAL ETHOS of Stevenson's rhyme has been greatly undermined by many recent studies of James's fiction. Finding the hidden agendas of police surveillance, reification, commodification, advertising, and the mass market in James's aesthetic, Jamesian criticism has plucked him from the heavens and planted him somewhat uneasily on the sordid terrain of earth.[1] Americanist scholarship of the last decade or so has deconstructed James's aesthetic retreat from the American landscape of consumer capitalism in order to reveal that his fiction participates in and unwittingly underwrites the economic order that he disdained. Like his fellow realists, James finds himself charged with having failed to construct a truly oppositional space for the American novel.

In many respects, however, this "failure" is not surprising. The freedom that James deemed essential for the novel in "The Art of Fiction"—"It lives upon exercise, and the very meaning of exercise is freedom"[2]—was not construed as an escape from all limits, but a freedom within certain necessary and desirable limits. Equating the novelist and the historian, James, in this 1884 essay, dissociates freedom from willfulness and caprice (hence his censure of Anthony Trollope for claiming that "he can give his narrative any turn the reader may like best") and places it instead within the demands

18

of a "sacred office . . . to represent and illustrate the past, the actions of men" (379,380). It is James's effort to locate aesthetic freedom within some framework mimetic of social relations that bears exploration here. As an inveterate aesthete who by the mid-1870s had decided to cast his lot abroad, James may seem, at first glance, a perverse choice for a consideration of the interrelation of race and literature during this period. Except for brief returns in the early 1880s, James stayed away from his homeland until 1904 when he was 61 years old—an absence which meant that his experience of the dramatic social changes in American society between Reconstruction and the turn of the century was heavily mediated. Nonetheless, as George Fredrickson points out, James's family during the Civil War years was deeply affected by the cause of black emancipation. The martyrdom of Robert Gould Shaw while leading the valiant but unsuccessful assault on Fort Wagner by the Massachusetts 54th Fifty-fourth Regiment, which except for its officers was all black, galvanized the "honest humanitarianism of the James family."[3] James's brothers, Wilkinson (Wilky), who served as an adjutant in the Fifty-fourth and was badly wounded in the attack on Fort Wagner, and Robertson, who also joined the Union Army ranks, serving for a time in a black regiment as well, were the active wartime participants in the James family. Henry, as he recalls in *Notes of a Son and Brother,* was despite his nonparticipation, caught up in the fervor: "our sympathies, our own as a family's, were, in the current phrase, all enlisted on behalf of the race that had sat in bondage."[4] Even before the war, James remembers being told of the escape of two slaves, Davy and Aunt Sylvia, whose owners, the Norcoms, were visiting from Kentucky. In regard to the escape, James's sentiments were smugly, if quietly, abolitionist: he recalls having taken "a vague little inward Northern comfort in [the Norcoms'] inability, in their discreet decision, not to raise the hue and cry."[5] And though the intensity of James's abolitionist sympathies waned, it would, given his background, be inappropriate to see James as entirely aloof from the political fate of black Americans before and after emancipation. In addition, during his lengthy expatriation, James's ongoing involvement with major American monthly and weekly publications through his fiction and criticism was one of several factors that made him a presence in the land of his birth, while making the social problems of American society an essential part of his aesthetic. From the end of the Civil War through the 1880s and 1890s, these magazines, which included *The Nation*, the *Atlantic Monthly, Century, Harper's Monthly,* and the *North American Review,* discussed and debated the "Negro Question."

Although one has to turn to the cultural critique James offers in such documents as *The American Scene* or his autobiographical works to find anything approaching a sustained focus on black Americans, the fiction and criticism James authored before his return to America suggest a continual interplay between black/white racial differences and literary aesthetics. Whether it is Mr. Touchett in *The Portrait of a Lady* saying, "Of course I talk like an American—I can't talk like a Hottentot," or Merton Densher's observation in *The Wings of the Dove* that in fulfilling their social obligations, Milly Theale, Kate Croy, Mrs. Stringham, and Mrs. Lowder "have been given up, like navvies or niggers, to real physical toil," references to race and ethnicity appear as almost "throwaway" remarks in many of James's fictions—colloquialisms that give to his narrative and dialogue an "air of reality."[6] These references, however, are not just marks of "reality" but important keys to some of James's major aesthetic preoccupations. Allusions to racial difference sometimes point to what James in his notebooks refers to as "the great question of *subject*," that is, the question of whether or not his American characters could provide the stuff of great fiction. Racial references also point to James's ongoing inquiry into the interrelation of aesthetic possibilities and social relations. For example, in *The American Scene* James accounted for the poor condition of Southern literature by pointing to the lingering effects of a slave society and to the "intimate presence of the negro." The social reality of African Americans had become a "prison of the Southern spirit" and James conjectured that "with an equal exposure" it would potentially prove limiting to him as well.[7] Though this view of the aesthetic liabilities of the black social presence is not fully articulated by James until *The American Scene,* it emerges in James's aesthetic in the early 1880s.

James's work also seems to fit into the prevailing climate of race relations in late nineteenth-century America, especially within the full-scale retreat of the North from support of black equal rights. The point here is not to arraign James on charges of bigotry and racism, nor to place on his doorstep primary or significant responsibility for the outrages committed against black Americans during these decades. Certainly one could build a case on James's racism and anti-Semitism, and his endorsement of views inhospitable to the equal rights demands of black Americans. The presentation of racial differences in James's later documents is often so invidious that in the words of Maxwell Geismar, "it almost appeared that Jews, Negroes and Lovers were the worst culprits in his *fin de siècle* scene of bohemian decadence."[8] Additionally, given the way that 1890s Reconstruction historiography helped to legitimate black disfranchisement, James's favorable review of W. A. Dunning's *Essays on the Civil War and Reconstruction* in 1898 is perhaps suspect. Noting that Dunning's essays tell a tale in which "the fond old figment of the Sovereign State . . . becomes for us a living, conscious figure, the protagonist of the epic," James grants a romantic status to the cause of states' rights under which the rights of African Americans were violently denied.[9]

One would, however, hesitate to credit James's review of Dunning with any significant role in establishing the legitimacy of the historian's scholarship; James reviews Dunning's collection from the standpoint of a layman. Also worth keeping in mind is that James's remarks on blacks in *The American Scene* did not make their appearance until after the disfranchisement and segregation of African Americans had been virtually completed. Southerners needed no encouragement or legitimation from an expatriate novelist. Moreover, *The American Scene* has been praised for its multicultural vision. William Boelhower, perhaps somewhat surprisingly, claims that in *The American Scene* "James is speaking on behalf of cultural diversity," employing a voice that derives from the fiction of his major phase in which "each work was a wholly new start, a wholly new attempt, to study shifting points of view and complex relations."[10] Certainly James's uses of terms like *ethnic synthesis* and his prediction in *The American Scene* that "the accent of the very ultimate future, in the States, may be destined to become the most beautiful on the globe and the very music of humanity . . . but whatever we shall know it for, certainly, we shall not know it for English—in any sense for which there is an existing literary measure" lends some credence to Boelhower's observation.[11] There is, in remarks like these, perhaps an indication of James's openness to the possibilities of American racial democracy. But John Higham is

probably more accurate in finding in *The American Scene* a patrician
"pessimism" and a "eulogistic" tone on behalf of the passing of Anglo-Saxon ideals.[12] At any rate, James's contribution to the discourse of race in America is at best ambivalent.

Where James's work, in fact, might be more helpful in a discussion of race in America lies along a slightly less direct path. The
construction of racial difference as a social problem for posteman-
cipation America depended at least in part on a "prior" imagination of public social interactions as versions of private intimacy. In
other words, when James in *The American Scene* refers to a public encounter with a group of African Americans in Washington, D.C., as
an example of the "thumping legacy of the intimate presence of
the negro," his remarks assume the intelligibility of this public encounter as somehow "intimate."[13] Certainly the construction of
public places as intimate spaces might be effectively explained as a
response to and a way of controlling racial and ethnic differences,
which is why *prior* appears here in quotation marks; but this construction of intimacy also drew upon other aesthetic and social assumptions which can shed additional light on how the threat of
"social equality" of black and white races could resonate so power-
fully in a nation that had by the mid-1880s all but foreclosed any
such possibility.

For James, as Carl Smith observes, the increasing accessibility of
foreign travel to white Americans was itself disconcerting. The
growth of tourism as an industry in the post Civil War years and
James's belief that "the once-exotic Old World had . . . pandered
to the sightseer and had thus cheapened itself" gave a negative cast
to James's attitudes towards his fellow citizens even when they were
of the same race: "The new travellers [James] saw were an unknown and ominous quantity in an unintelligible world. To his eye
they were incomprehensible and void of comprehension themselves, without any taste or standards to judge what they were viewing."[14] Social practice permitted, even encouraged, the cultured
observer to question, if only tacitly, the right of other Americans to
avail themselves of the privileges that ought to be reserved for
those having the capacity to appreciate finer things. Black Americans who sought to enter the public sphere as potential equals
would necessarily be met by a social challenge; their unchecked
entry into spaces previously felt to be exclusive would quite readily
be seen as an index of a social order well on the way to decline. As

a result, while "one would be quite as likely to meet a cow or a
horse in American drawing-room as a person of color" (to quote a
character from William Dean Howells's *An Imperative Duty*),[15] advocates for black political equality nonetheless found themselves
again and again having to deny the charge that they were promoting social equality.

When brought by Southern conservatives, such charges were
clearly opportunistic, calculated to play upon the fears of an
American public that through the 1870s had dealt with the shocks
of immigration, labor unrest, and economic panics. But the fact
that these charges "worked" is an indication that they somehow
made sense to Americans, many of whom had no day-to-day contact with black Americans. Despite obvious economic, legal, and
social barriers between African Americans and other Americans,
other factors were at work. In Higham's words, "the twin ideals of
a common humanity and of equal rights continued in the 1870's
and 1880's to foster faith in assimilation. Temporarily the tasks of
postwar reconstruction even widened assimilationist ideals; for the
Radical Republicans' effort to redeem the southern Negro, to
draw him within the pale of the state, and to weld the two races into
a homogeneous nationality discouraged emphasis on basic human
differences."[16] Faith in these ideals was not continuous and did not
at any time fully displace doubts and antidemocratic tendencies.
But what such ideals did emphasize was that the logic of democracy
made difficult the drawing of social and political boundaries between races. As Bishop T. U. Dudley, writing in *Century* magazine,
averred: "I can find no reason to believe that the great races into
which humanity is divided shall remain forever distinct, with their
race-marks of color and of form. Centuries hence the red man, the
yellow, the white, and the black may all have ceased to exist as such,
and in America be found the race combining the bloods of them
all."[17] Although the telos of racial amalgamation was never widely
embraced, it could readily be derived from the principles of equality. As novelists like James plunged into the task of representing
Americans, they, too, had to confront the implications of democracy for the shaping of the novel.

II

In order to see the ways in which the social meaning of race played
into James's aesthetic, it helps to remember that in much of his

criticism and fiction he almost obsessively seeks social correlatives for aesthetic concerns: the novelist is compared to a pawnbroker; *ficelles* are described as "the fishwives who helped to bring back to Paris from Versailles, on that ominous day of the first half of the French Revolution, the carriage of the royal family";[18] and the need for criticism is likened to the practice of discriminating among passengers in railway cars.[19] In fact, James's willingness to draw his metaphors for his craft as much from the realm of social relations as from the realms of "nature" or other art forms may be one of the signatures of James's realism. But while James's fiction may proceed from "real life" and from the actions of actual individuals, his writings tend to push the boundaries of the real. As he suggests in his preface to *The Ambassadors*, "for development, for expression of its maximum, my glimmering story was, at the earliest stage, to have nipped the thread of connexion with the possibilities of the actual reported speaker."[20] The real world possibilities of his subject are transmuted into possibilities for the artist.

Notwithstanding his desires to "nip the thread of connection" to the actual, the power of much of James's work derives from its acknowledgement of how difficult it is to bring about such transformations. Obstacles to aesthetic transformations arise in good measure because James cannot escape the belief that the actual world of social relations "matters." For example, although the appeal to freedom in "The Art of Fiction" is made on behalf of the novel, it extends, however briefly, to the social status of the aspiring writer. In response to Walter Besant's injunction that "'a writer whose friends and personal experiences belong to the lower middle-class should carefully avoid introducing his characters into society,'" James recoils, observing that Besant's "remark about the lower middle-class writer and his knowing his place is perhaps rather chilling" (386–87). While James's protest against Besant's class prejudice is itself "perhaps rather" mild, it does register an awareness that James's aesthetic position may have political implications. And though his demurral at class snobbery lets stand for the moment Besant's strictures on the woman novelist—"'a young lady brought up in a quiet country village should avoid descriptions of garrison life'" (386)—James's account of the artistic faculty of receiving direct impressions challenges Besant even on this question. In recalling the successful portrait of French Protestant youth drawn by an English "woman of genius," James explains that she had got her direct personal impression, and she turned out her type. . . . Above all, however, she was blessed with the faculty which when you give it an inch takes an ell, and which for the artist is a much greater source of strength than any accident of residence or of place in the social scale. The power to guess the unseen from the seen, to trace the implication of things, to judge the whole piece by the pattern, the condition of feeling life in general so completely that you are well on your way in knowing any particular corner of it—this cluster of gifts may almost be said to constitute experience, and they occur in country and in town, and in the most differing stages of education. (389)

As described here, the novelistic consciousness couples a disdain for class barriers with a belief in a quasi-democratic distribution of talent, potentially paving the way for an argument on behalf of the social rise or inclusion of previously excluded groups.

James's remarks emerge from a context in which the social distribution of consciousness and feeling was racially and politically inflected. Although it would be impossible to treat this matter fully in the space I have here (I give the issue more extensive treatment in my third chapter), nineteenth-century progressive social reform often depended on the possibility of acknowledging the consciousness, feelings, and the "reality of . . . suffering" of the oppressed.[21] Antebellum sentimental fiction had done a great deal to assert the reality of the suffering of the slave, countering in this way the view that the black slave could "scarcely feel his own calamitous situation"—a remark made by Alexis De Tocqueville, who, perhaps not coincidentally, is the favorite author of Basil Ransom, the hero of James's *The Bostonians*.[22] Whatever the success of abolitionist fiction during the antebellum period, however, the proper feelings toward emancipated African Americans or other darker races seemed a different matter.

Various observers, among them William James and W. E. B. Du Bois, noted with alarm the political consequences for the United States in failing to attribute to others the capacity to feel. In one of his turn-of-the-century protests against American imperialism, William James observed that "there is no clear sign of its ever having occurred to anyone at Washington that the Filipinos could have any feeling or insides of their own whatever that might possibly need to be considered in our arrangements. It was merely a big material corporation against a small one, the 'soul' of the big one consisting in a stock of moral phrases, the little one owning no soul at all."[23] As James makes plain, the denial of feeling and consciousness functions here as a justification for imperialist depredations. Human and spiritual regard all flow from a willingness to acknowledge the emotional capacities of others. Justice demands, in the words of W. E. B. Du Bois, that we not "forget that each unit in the mass is a throbbing human soul. Ignorant it may be, and poverty stricken, black and curious in limb and ways and thought; and yet it loves and hates, it toils and tires, it laughs and weeps its bitter tears, and looks in vague and awful longing at the grim horizon of its life,—all this, even as you and I."[24] To bring to light the humanity of the downtrodden and their capacity to feel was to make a claim for their innate equality with the observer. The differences in the social status of the observed and the observer then are revealed as misalignments in the social order which might be exploited to challenge the legitimacy of that order. Individuals who feel unjustly deprived of the wherewithal to realize their potentials might become sources of, or parties to, social unrest, as is the case with Hyacinth Robinson of *The Princess Casamassima,* a youth in the terms of "The Art of Fiction" "on whom nothing was lost."[25]

Hyacinth's ineffectual career as a revolutionary, however, is instructive: James's fictional interest in such misalignments stems primarily from the opportunities they create for dramatizing the turmoils of a consciousness aware of its plight. As James puts the matter in the preface to *The Wings of the Dove* the "supremely touching value" is "to be the heir of all ages only to know yourself, as that consciousness should deepen, balked of your inheritance."[26] The tragedy of the individual situation is almost a given. The social tensions in James's work tend to cash out as individual knowledge rather than social change.

Nonetheless such tensions retain their social explosiveness. The distribution of consciousness or the ability to feel one's situation plays a role for James in determining which individuals can serve as appropriate fictional subjects, an issue, which Charles Feidelson points out, began intensely to preoccupy James during the years surrounding the composition of *The Portrait of a Lady.*[27] At times James suggests that the decision regarding the appropriateness of subject is a foregone conclusion—that there are individuals who innately possess or lack the capacity to feel their situation. For the writer, the latter individuals are best avoided because "we care, our curiosity and our sympathy care, comparatively little for what happens to the stupid, the coarse and the blind." Those about whom we care are, in turn, "capable of feeling . . . more than another of what is to be felt."[28] The author's job is to locate those capable of feeling.

At other times, though, James seems to say that fictional representation itself is not merely a way of locating such consciousnesses, but a way of distributing awareness, of "*imputing* . . . intelligence.*" That is, in some of his formulations James suggests that representation does not merely reflect preexisting consciousness but that it creates or imputes consciousness. He writes in the preface to *The Princess Casamassima* that:

> My report of people's experience—my report as a "storyteller"—is essentially my appreciation of it, and there is no "interest" for me in what my hero, my heroine or any one else does save through that admirable process. As soon as I begin to appreciate simplification is imperilled: the sharply distinguished parts of any adventure, any case of endurance and performance, melt together as an appeal. I then see their "doing", that of the persons just mentioned, as, immensely, their feeling, their feeling as their doing; since I can have none of the conveyed sense and taste of their situation without becoming intimate with them. I can't be intimate without that sense and taste, and I can't appreciate save by intimacy, any more than I can report save by a projected light. Intimacy with a man's specific behaviour, with his given case, is desperately certain to make us see it as a whole—in which event arbitrary limitations of our vision lose whatever beauty they may on occasion have pretended to.

Inasmuch as "intimacy" and feeling derive from the author's appreciation, the distinctions that James wishes to draw between the "really sentient" and the "persons of markedly limited sense" become threatened.[29] A character's availability for representation potentially draws her within the scope of the author's appreciation and opens the way for the possibility of sentience and intimate relation. The character seems to make a demand for human regard, despite the author's initial designs. Such is the problem posed by

Henrietta Stackpole in *The Portrait of a Lady*. James, as he says in the preface to the novel, envisioned her as part of the treatment, but over the course of the novel she seems to become so much more than that.

Compounding the uncertainty in the author's relation to his subject is that the process seems reversible. Not only can characters whose function is to aid the novel's presentation make a demand to be considered as its focus but the "subject" can slide almost imperceptibly back into the "treatment." The problem, James complains, of focusing a novel on the "slimnesses" of "young girls" is that with the young American girl at the center of the text there is always the threat that the story will become less a chronicle of her destiny than an investigation of other destinies. Or in James's words, the center will be usurped by "a hundred other persons, made of much stouter stuff, and each involved moreover in a hundred relations which matter to *them* concomitantly with that one."[30] As a result, those characters whose role is to serve primarily as props seem to become actors, while the central actor tends to become a prop. The solution to his dilemma, James averred in the preface to *The Portrait of a Lady*, was to "'place the centre of the subject in the young woman's own consciousness'" (10)—the stuff of that novel would not be the woman's relationship with others but her consciousness of those relationships. Given, however, that the plot depends greatly on Isabel's not being conscious or aware of what is going on around her for a significant portion of the story, even this solution was somewhat tenuous.

In the text, then, James works through his misgivings about the ability of Isabel, his subject, to hold the novel's center. And as a sign of the novel's Americanness, these misgivings occasionally take the form of racial markings. For example, when Mrs. Touchett responds to Henrietta Stackpole's championing of American women by saying that American ladies are "the slaves of slaves . . . the companions of their servants—the Irish chambermaid and the negro waiter. They share their work" (89), she is not only slighting the capacities of American women and servants, but is also lodging a complaint against James's fictional subject itself. *The Portrait of a Lady*, focused as it is on "the slaves of slaves" may be in its own way slightly vulgar; it is in some sense simply a tale of a woman who makes a bad marriage. But for James, rescuing his subject from vulgarity, or keeping it from "vulgar hands" becomes the drama of the novel, a drama in which the social markings of race become crucial.

The overwhelming success of *The Portrait of a Lady*—its status as a classic of American literature and the general acknowledgment of Isabel Archer as one of that literature's more memorable heroines—has perhaps occluded the very dynamics that make the experience of the book's "achievement" possible. Being too ready to credit Isabel's superiority is to commit the error of her less astute "contemporaries" whom the narrator describes as all too willing to allow Isabel to "pass . . . for a young woman of extraordinary profundity" without being precisely able to say why (53). By contrast, a proper assessment of Isabel's "value" must proceed through the narrator's admission that his heroine's "errors and delusions were frequently such as a biographer interested in preserving the dignity of his subject must shrink from specifying" (53). There is a difference, if you will, between speaking well of Isabel Archer (which most everyone at the beginning of the novel quite easily does) and in learning (as the reader presumably will by the tale's end) why one must not speak ill of James's heroine. Isabel must fulfill the type of the somewhat vulgar American heiress who would be "an easy victim of scientific criticism" before she can transcend that type and become the novel's true center who can "awaken on the reader's part an impulse more tender and more purely expectant" (54).

It is with a project like this in view that James, in *The Portrait of a Lady*, and in many of his works, constructs a plot that mandates the manipulation of characters by others. Individual figures are put at the service of others, made available for use. The freedom achieved by these characters, then, derives not so much from an ability to avoid manipulation, which is unavoidable, but rather from an ability to see the social design made possible by their use by others. Having perceived the nature of the design into which they've been drawn, James's protagonists can then participate in a grander revision of that design. The Isabel Archers, Lambert Strethers, and the Maisies do not renounce the manipulation of others; they seek to turn these manipulations to higher ends. The failure to have another horizon in sight is to risk becoming vulgar.

Part of the drama played out in *The Portrait of a Lady* turns on the quality of service that Isabel will provide. Her inability throughout most of the novel to see the plot within which she is embedded, or, to use the Countess Gemini's words, her ability "to succeed in not knowing" what is going on around her, consigns her for a time to vulgar usage. It is perhaps somewhat paradoxical that Osmond, despite the obviousness of his evil, censures her justly. Isabel *is* a bit vulgar, and upon discovering the full measure of the way she has been manipulated, she is brought to face "the dry staring fact that she had been an applied handled hung-up tool, as senseless and convenient as mere shaped wood and iron" (459). Having insisted upon her possession of the qualities of agency—the right to judge and to choose—Isabel discovers that she has been merely an object manipulated by other agents. Subsequent to this discovery she explains to Mrs. Touchett her dislike of Madame Merle by saying that her husband's former lover had "made a convenience of me," confirming in this respect Mrs. Touchett's earlier lament about American ladies (475).

Throughout the novel, Mrs. Touchett often acts as an internal critic of James's subject, assessing Isabel's capacities and decisions, and commenting acerbically on the author's "ado" about his heroine. Seeing in her niece both potential for improvement and folly, and seeing in Isabel's willingness to lavish her grand conceptions and wealth on someone who "has no importance" (283), a capacity for great error, Mrs. Touchett delineates not only Isabel's risks but also the thin line that James must walk between writing a novel that is much ado about nothing and creating a portrait whose subject justifies its treatment. Mrs. Touchett tells Isabel's story accurately if badly—without appreciation and nuance—leaving it for James to tell it well.

Ultimately, what makes Isabel a fit subject for portraiture in James's scheme is her eventual awareness of her situation, her ability finally to see where she is and to become more than a mere convenience. It is Isabel's vision that effectively exiles Madame Merle to America to become an American lady, in contrast to Isabel, whose nationality is not mentioned in the book's title. Isabel is simply "a lady." Thus, by the end of the novel, Isabel has defied Mrs. Touchett's description of "poor American ladies." For Isabel to be regarded as a subject is for her *not* to be the companion of an Irish chambermaid or a black waiter—that fate is to be reserved for the Serena Merles of the world. Isabel's destiny lies elsewhere. And in convincing us that it does, James has also made another point: the

degree to which Mrs. Touchett's censure of American ladies seems
not to fit James's heroine is precisely the degree to which black
waiters and Irish chambermaids could not possess the qualities
that make Isabel a lady fit for portraiture.
Of course not all of James's candidates for representation experience like success. The lady and gentleman who seek employment
as models in the 1892 story "The Real Thing" are able "only [to]
show themselves, clumsily, for the fine, clean, well-groomed animals that they were," and are unable to function as appropriate
subjects for representation. And as the story's narrator describes
these "well-groomed animals" who signify "everlasting English
amateurishness" he invokes black racial difference. When asked to
assess the potential usefulness of the displaced gentlefolk, who are
pompously named the Monarchs, the narrator remarks, "it was an
embarrassment to find myself appraising physically, as if they were
animals on hire or useful blacks, a pair which I should have expected to meet only in one of the relations in which criticism is
tacit."[31] The displacement of social relations by physical appraisal
as figured not only in the equation of the Monarchs to blacks, but
both to beasts is inimical to social and aesthetic ease. The narrator
cannot make the Monarchs work into his illustrations, and when
they seek to become his servants instead he cannot bear to watch
them perform this role. Inasmuch as the narrator finds it impossible to create successful sketches of the Monarchs, who do, however, lend themselves quite well to being photographed, artistic
representation becomes a social, intangible, imaginative process
rather than a physical, mechanical, mimetic one. The painter's servants—Miss Churm and Oronte—make better models because
they so easily become other than they are (ladies, gentlemen, and
so on), while being socially precisely what they are (servants).
     In some respects, James's references to race are gratuitous. Nei-
ther The Portrait of a Lady nor "The Real Thing" would seem to depend on evoking black racial presence; neither tale, if you will ex-
cuse the phrasing, is peppered with references to black racial
difference. But the superfluous invocation of racial difference
helps reveal the way that for James the art of fiction is always a re-
flection on the social conditions necessary for sustaining fiction as
high art. In considering the aesthetic possibilities of his subjects,
references to black racial difference were recurring signs of

James's misgivings about the novel, his various subjects, and the aesthetic possibilities of his homeland. To gauge the degree to which this is so, we can turn to an experimental short story written at about the time that Isabel's trials were being put before James's readers. "The Point of View" which was begun in Washington during James's brief visits to the United States in the early 1880s, has been described by Leon Edel as "a series of folding mirrors, capturing in a bright critical light the glittering weaknesses of the American democracy."[32] Within the story, however, the most dramatic shocks at the vulgarity of democracy are registered on a racial and ethnic scale.

This tale comprises eight letters to friends and relatives written by seven characters who have recently arrived in the United States from abroad. Among the group are five Americans: Aurora Church and her mother, who have returned in hopes of making a marriage for the young girl in her native land; Louis Leverett, a fastidious young expatriate in love with Paris; Marcellus Cockerel, a well-travelled young man glad to be back home; and Miss Sturdy, an even-tempered woman of fifty. Rounding out the group are Edward Antrobus, a radical British Member of Parliament, and Gustave Lejaune, a French academician.

Inasmuch as the tale exhibits a plot, it is the desire and failure of Aurora Church to reenter American society and find a husband. Her letters both begin and end the story, and two of the other characters figure briefly as potential suitors. The failed matrimonial quest is only a pretext, however; Aurora Church is not overly devastated by her failure, except that it may eventually force her return to Europe. The story's chief interest lies in the differing perspectives on American democracy offered by the various correspondents, responses which ostensibly run the gamut of possible opinion. Leverett, Lejaune, and Mrs. Church are horrified by what democracy appears to mean; Aurora and Antrobus are alternately intrigued and discomfited by the unfamiliar society; Miss Sturdy, the older woman, responds to the scene in an equable manner; and Mr. Cockerel waxes jingoistic in his crowing about American superiority. Despite these differences in opinion, however, all of the observers seem to agree on some basic facts. America features an abundance of young pretty women, while lacking aesthetic distinctions, manners, outward signs of social authority, and attentive servants.

That is, the fragmented points of view disagree less on what America is than on how to feel about it, or, as James foresaw the tale in his notebooks, it was to be a "description of a situation, or incident, in an alternation of letters, written from an aristocratic, and a democratic, point of view;—both enlightened and sincere."³³ Cockerel's description of the District of Columbia agrees essentially with Lejaune's in terms of the facts. The chief differences are affective. Cockerel writes to his sister that the Capitol was notably accessible: "The doors were gaping wide—I walked all about; there were no doorkeepers, no officers, nor flunkeys,—not even a policeman to be seen." In his turn, Lejaune observes of the Capitol, "You go into the Capitol as you would into a railway station; you walk about as you would in the Palais Royal. No functionaries, no door-keepers, no officers, no uniforms, no badges, no restrictions, no authority."³⁴

That the observations echo each other is readily apparent. Both men remark the ease of access and the absence of officials. But Lejaune's views register distaste. The railway station is the image that James himself seizes on in the 1893 "Criticism" essay to signal the demoralization of critical practice, complaining that "we blunder in and out of the affair [criticism] as if it were a railway station— the easiest and most public of the arts."³⁵ Like James, Lejaune objects strenuously to the promiscuous and unchallenged access that seems available for all who would enter America's public and discursive spaces. He agrees with James that some discrimination is necessary if one is to establish, in Lejaune's words, "national dignity" (593).

Their differing opinions on America aside, Lejaune and Cockerel focus on the outward social manifestations of democracy rather than on political questions in constructing their accounts of America. "I don't even care for the political" (592), Lejaune tells his correspondent, while Cockerel tells his sister that "the questions of the future are social questions" (599). Cockerel then opposes these social questions to "petty politics" (598). The displacement of political critique by aesthetic and social observations not only reflects the general disillusionment that many American elites felt toward politics during this period but also signals how difficult it was, within the discourse of the realistic novel of manners to find a space for political discussion. To Cockerel, politics means "European jealousies and rivalries" (599); to Lejaune, the

American political machine "operates very roughly, and some day, evidently, it will explode" (592). From either side, the representation of politics is problematic.

In describing the representation of Washington that James gives in *The American Scene* about a quarter of a century after the publication of "The Point of View," Mark Seltzer has noted that what is "particularly interesting about James's account of the nation's political capital . . . is the radical displacement or 'general elimination' of the signs of power. . . . in *The American Scene* the nominal or official site of power presents only a vague blank." Seltzer sees this absence of politics as part of James's "aestheticizing of power," an observation that Seltzer makes in the context challenging those critics who would see James's works as occupying a place "outside" the structures of power. What one needs to note about "The Point of View" is that the absence of "official" Washington from the characters' accounts does not mark an "art of omission and suppression"[36] that James's admires in diplomatic Washington and wishes to recapitulate in his representational practices. Rather, the absence of official Washington here is meant to mark the democratic empowerment of the individual on the American scene. As Cockerel exclaims, "In fact there's no government at all to speak of; it seems too good to be true. The first day I was here I went to the Capitol, and it took me ever so long to figure to myself that I had as good a right there as anyone else—that the whole magnificent pile (it *is* magnificent, by the way) was in fact my own" (602–3). This sense of individual ownership and the individual right of access to the seat of power was part of a dissolving of "the external restraints on individual achievement. It was an article of faith that this land of opportunity had leveled all the barriers to individual mobility."[37] The America that James and his fictional travelers confronted in 1881 was one that could, despite evidence to the contrary, still sing the power of the individual. Additionally, the America that James visited in 1881 and 1882 was an America that had not yet officially invalidated the 1875 Civil Rights Act, which provided that

> all persons within the jurisdiction of the United States shall
> be entitled to the full and equal enjoyment of the accommo-
> dations, advantages, facilities, and privileges of inns, public
> conveyances on land or water, theatres, and other places of

public amusement; subject only to the conditions and limitations established by law, and applicable alike to citizens of every race and color, regardless of any previous condition of servitude.[38]

Legally, then, the right of access and ownership that Cockerel celebrates was within the reach of African Americans as well. Thus the vision of America that hovers within sight of "The Point of View" was a vision of the meaning of racial democracy. Perhaps not surprisingly, as James recalls in the New York Edition preface to the story, the "slightly sordid tenement" of his Washington muse was suffused by the presence of race:

> I had had "rooms" in it, and I could remember how the rooms, how the whole place, a nest of rickety tables and chairs, lame and disqualified utensils of every sort, and of smiling, shuffling, procrastinating persons of colour, had exhaled for me, to pungency, the domestic spirit of the "old South." I had nursed the unmistakable scent; I had read history by its aid; I had learned more than I could say of what had anciently been the matter under the reign of the great problem of persons of colour—so badly the matter, by my vision, that a deluge of blood and fire and tears had been needed to correct it.[39]

Even within the veils of aesthetic recall, the story emerges as a form of racial/political commentary. Though the tale takes place aboard ship, in Boston, and in Washington, D.C., it is the District of Columbia that stands out in James's memory. And though the story is about a variety of characters, "persons of colour" populate the mise en scène of James's reminiscence. The "racial" note is sounded clearly. And the story takes up directly "the reign of the great problem of persons of colour," problems that manifest themselves in the text. Thus tracing the politics of the text cannot be adequately achieved by mapping the course of its evasions. "The Point of View" must be met more or less head-on.

The other key difference in the accounts of Washington given by Lejaune and Cockerel is that Lejaune, in his criticism, notices what is absent in Cockerel's praise but evident in James's recollection: Washington's sizeable black population. The notice, of course, is invidious. Lejaune conveys the capital's lack of architectural dis-

tinction by saying, "this is the principal seat, but, save for three or
four big buildings, most of them *affreux* it looks like a settlement of
negroes" (592). Critics of Radical Reconstruction and of the subsequent Republican administrations often decried the vulgarization of the period, pointing to an alleged predominance of the African presence in federal government. Interestingly, among D.C.'s
black inhabitants during the period of James's visit was Frederick
Douglass, who had served through March 1881 as Federal Marshall
of the District of Columbia and, in fact, had led the procession during the inauguration of James A. Garfield. By the time of James's
visit, Douglass was no longer marshall but had been appointed Re-
corder of Deeds for the District of Columbia. These historical
notes do not enter in to "The Point of View," but in the story the
debasement of American public life is figured most graphically by
the noticing of blacks on the social scene. Lejaune and Leverett,
the two correspondents who censure American society most severely, point up the absence of taste and refinement by noticing racial and ethnic differences.

Though his observations focus on Boston rather than Washington, Leverett's account of the social scene is much like the French
academician's. Arriving at his hotel, he finds himself in the hands
of a "savage Irishman," and once in the dining room he is attended
by black servants:

> The servants are black and familiar; their faces shine as they
> shuffle about; there are blue tones in their dark masks. They
> have no manners; they address you, but they don't answer
> you; they plant themselves at your elbow (it rubs their clothes
> as you eat), and watch you as if your proceedings were
> strange. They deluge you with iced water. . . . If you read the
> newspaper,—which I don't, gracious Heaven! I can't,—they
> hang over your shoulder and peruse it also. I always fold it up
> and present it to them; the newspapers here are indeed for
> an African taste. (584)

In his xenophobic rantings Leverett associates black Americans
with a lack of manners, discretion, and social regard. An "African
taste" is clearly a lack of taste, and Leverett's relinquishing of the
paper is not an act of generosity but an attempt to avoid intimacy.
Leverett's inability to interpret the "excessive" attentions of black
servants and their desire to read the paper (which as the history of

African-American literacy tells us is laden with social significance) as other than rudeness and incompetence evinces the "lack of reciprocity" that James found endemic to bourgeois society in general and to American society in particular. The link between the lack of personal service and the lack of reciprocity is emblemized, first by the black servants—"they address you but don't answer you"—and then by the "speaking tube" in Leverett's hotel room, which in desperation he fills "with incoherent sounds, and sounds more incoherent yet come back to me" (585). He fails to make his wants understood. In general, he does not "feel at all *en rapport*" (586).

Remarkable in this story of seven correspondents is the lack of any return correspondence. The eight letters are sent to people who do not answer. The characters enjoy some brief intercourse among themselves, but it is halting and short-lived. From the first, social connections are aborted. Aurora writes that her mother desires to make the acquaintance of Lejaune: "She always makes a little vague inclination, with a smile, when he passes her, and he answers with a respectful bow; but it goes no further to mamma's disappointment" (546). Miss Sturdy extends an invitation to Mr. Antrobus for a visit, but is not taken up. Later the connections that are made are simply dropped. Leverett speaks of Aurora as if she has joined the ranks of the dead: "I have lost her now; I am sorry, because she liked to listen to me. She has passed away; I shall not see her again" (587). And Aurora herself complains that Mr Leverett and Mr Cockerel "disappeared one fine day, without the smallest pretension to having broken my heart" (606). Perhaps frighteningly for James, the principals of his story who "address" one another without answering behave just like the black servants.

The fragmentation signaled by the multiple points of view in this story is not a radically fragmented reality but a society without reciprocity. As indicated above, some of the characters do experience a degree of ease and elation in their encounters with American society, but these encounters have no racial or ethnic content. Cockerel, Antrobus and Miss Sturdy all have relatively positive interactions with Americans of different orders but record no racial differences. To see American democracy as even slightly palatable one must see it as homogenous. By contrast, those characters who find American society the most inhospitable, intolerable, and intrusive tend to mark their distaste with ethnic and racial notices. For these characters the mark of the most vulgarly unresponsive

consciousness is the African American, a figure whose presence
must be suppressed for any sense of social ease.

III

What this reading of "The Point of View" also suggests are the troubling links between James's treatment of ethnicity and race and
the nation's general acquiescence to laws mandating the separation of races in American public spaces. James's work (and American realism in general) must be read against the backdrop of the
North's retreat from a commitment to securing freedom and
equal rights for black Americans—a retreat that moved the body of
Northern public opinion to an acceptance of policies and decisions mandating the social, political, and economic subordination
of the nation's freedmen. The de jure empowerment of African
Americans enhanced by the Civil Rights Act of 1866, the Four-
teenth Amendment, and the Civil Rights Act of 1875 was severely
crippled by the Supreme Court decision in what came to be known
as the *Civil Rights Cases,* a decision handed down in 1883, the year
following the publication of James's story in *Century* magazine.

That James strikes the racial note in the ways he does in these
tales points up the depth of, and the obliqueness of, his textual en-
gagement with racial debates of the period. Despite the problems
of reception that James would have with his American audience
throughout his career (*The Portrait of a Lady* was well received, but,
as might be expected, "The Point of View" was roundly criticized
by his readers),[40] on at least one key point the anxieties evident in
his fiction and criticism seemed to mirror the anxieties in American society at large: the seeming impossibility in reconciling "high"
cultural aims with a society that recognized blacks as equals.

The discomfort expressed by Lejaune and Leverett at the "African" presence on the American social scene was more than a species of the discomfort that many white Americans expressed when
justifying the enforcement of Jim Crow laws. Racial discomfort in
James's fiction also signaled the difficulty that American racial liberals would encounter in their efforts to redefine American social
space so that civil and social rights could be distinguished from
one another. Social relations, according to George Washington
Cable, were a matter of personal choice and not subject to un-
wanted encroachment. A man and woman attending a concert together, though "outnumbered a thousand to one, need not yield a

pennyweight of social interchange with any third person unless they so choose." Cable reasoned that "the principles of this case are not disturbed by any multiplication of the number of persons concerned, or by reading for concert hall either theater or steamboat or railway station or coach or lecture hall or streetcar or public library, or by supposing the social pair to be English, Turk, Jap, Cherokee, Ethiopian, Mexican, or 'American.'" The aggregation of racial groups in public did not portend "*social chaos.*"[41]

For James, however, individual interactions on American social space often manifested themselves as an assault on the personal relation—an assault redoubled by racial differences. Lejaune, Leverett, and Mrs. Touchett are mouthpieces for a discomfort that James himself later admits feeling in *The American Scene* when he finds that his "ease of contemplation of the subject" was "threatened" by the "thumping legacy of the intimate presence of the negro"[42] And his response to the "threat" of social intimacy was apparently indicative of prevailing attitudes towards the problem of social intimacy. The first number of the *American Journal of Sociology* asserted in July 1895 that "*the fact of human association is more obtrusive and relatively more influential than in any previous epoch. . . .* Men are more definitely and variously aware of each other than before. They are also more promiscuously perplexed by each other's presence."[43] It was being taken as a given that public association was not inherently benign, but something that must be taken into account scientifically, and perhaps legally and politically.

Although an air of national confidence prevailed through the 1870s,[44] these years also saw a "shift of ideological focus [that] produced a major political realignment, involving the foreclosure of Reconstruction and of government sponsorship of liberal reform, and the rejection of the democratic and perfectionist ideology that underlay those reforms in favor of an ideology protective of the power and status of industrial capitalists and managers."[45] Thus it is crucial to see that by the 1880s and 1890s arguments for desegregating American public space depended less upon utopian beliefs in an egalitarian democracy and more upon the pragmatic task of convincing Americans that public contact with individuals of different races was innocuous and beyond the reasonable policing power of state legislatures. In the words of Samuel Phillips, who submitted a brief on behalf of Homer Plessy in the landmark *Plessy* v. *Ferguson* decision, "color" did not place "men within the operation of the laws of *police*" while they traveled on common carriers.[46] The social contact created by association on trains, ships, and streetcars did not constitute a "social relation" and hence did not challenge communal norms regarding marriage, the family, and education. Civil equality did not presume social equality.

Ultimately, however, such arguments failed to persuade the courts and the American people that American public space should be integrated nationwide, and certain shadings in James's critical voice suggests that he, too, may have contributed to the chorus of voices providing a counterargument. That is, to the extent that Constitutional sanction of the Supreme Court's "separate but equal" decision in *Plessy* v. *Ferguson* needed "grounds for concluding that racial separation was 'reasonable' in the sense of arguably conducing to maintenance of public health, welfare, and morals,"[47] James's work offered no demurral. Again and again, James's writing suggests that cultural health depends on the ability to make discriminations that were social as well as aesthetic. In "Criticism" he likened critical essays to passengers on a train and warned that literature, "like other sensitive organisms, . . . is highly susceptible of demoralization . . . and the consequence of its keeping bad company is that it loses all heart."[48] Only three states had laws on the books mandating Jim Crow waiting rooms in railway stations by 1899, six years after the publication of James's essay.[49]

That James's discriminations in his essay were made on behalf of the novel without mention of race makes them all the more important for our purposes. Successful defenses of segregative legislation tended to disavow any prejudicial intent toward blacks as a justification. Instead, supporters of segregation argued the "reasonableness" of racial separation by pointing to the general societal acceptance of public carriers' provision of differentiated service in regard to sex, character, and deportment. The need for differentiation and discrimination is clearly indicated in James's essay. And though James's remarks on railway stations are made during his twenty-year absence from his native land, his attitudes about American public space and racial mingling were taking shape during the 1880s and 1890s when, according to Charles Lofgren, a "proliferation of police measures . . . contributed to the climate supporting judicial approval of racial segregation." During these decades state police power was extended by judicial decisions supporting the state's regulatory power over public and private realms provided that such uses of power could be construed as "reasonable" attempts to "promote public health, welfare and morals."[50] By the late 1890s laws mandating segregation in public places were widely seen as reasonable measures to promote public morals, and the attitudes expressed by James and some of his characters were in accord.

Jamesian narrative technique, however, did not merely underscore the dangers of failing to discriminate properly. Additionally, and somewhat paradoxically, it underscored the difficulty of making discriminations at all. In a social environment in which "reasonable" responses to race were those that acknowledged natural boundaries, the realistic novel carried a disruptive message. Even as civil rights advocates of the 1880s declared that "social equality is a fool's dream,"[51] realistic novels insisted on investigating the social implications of democracy, revealing how tenuous was any guarantee that racial liberals might offer. Realism, in fact, threatened to demolish the distinctions between civil and social rights so that within the purview of realistic fiction social and civil equality became hardly distinguishable from one another. In offering a criticism of E. L. Godkin's *Unforeseen Tendencies of Democracy* James writes, "One feels it to be a pity that, in such a survey, the reference to the social conditions as well should not somehow be interwoven: at so many points are they—whether for contradiction, confirmation, attenuation, or aggravation—but another aspect of the political."[52]

The imputed potential of realism to alter human relationships (or to underscore how human relationships were being altered) was often articulated in terms of the novel's ability to locate resemblance or commonality among people. Commenting on the implications of modern realism's ability to capitalize upon randomness, Erich Auerbach observed that "it is precisely the random moment which is comparatively independent of the controversial and unstable orders over which men fight and despair; it passes unaffected by them, as daily life. The more it is exploited, the more the elementary things which our lives have in common come to light. The more numerous, varied, and simple the people are who appear as subjects of such random moments, the more effectively must what they have in common shine forth."[53] The Howellsian echoes in Auerbach's prognosis are inescapable; realism presages

the democratization of human life, and the realist is the harbinger
of change: "He feels in every nerve the equality of things and the
unity of men."[54]

Of course, by focusing on the "insignificant" and the "random"
Howells and Auerbach made them precisely other than what they
claimed them to be. Rather than having located stable and uncon-
troversial bits of reality, Howells and Auerbach had noted how
thoroughly politicized such moments had become. During the realist era, however, no effective political discourse existed for articulating the political legitimacy of such moments. According to Irving Howe, for example, during this period "ideology is sometimes
treated by the American novelists as if it were merely a form of private experience. . . . Personalizing everything, they could bril-
liantly observe how social and individual experience melt into one
another so that the deformations of the one soon become the deformations of the other."[55] These mutual deformations meant that
even as George Washington Cable sought to assure his fellow
Southerners that "our persistent mistaking [the Negro's] civil
rights for social claims . . . was the taproot of the whole trouble,"[56]
the logic of realism suggested that Cable's foes were not at all mis-
taken. Although the segregated communities of the late twentieth
century illustrate graphically how resistant American social life has
been to civil rights demands, observers of postbellum American
public life could find little room to distinguish between political
and social claims. In the South the new social order created by
emancipation threw into question the whole array of interpersonal, interracial interactions. Everyday ceremonies of greeting
and courtesy became fraught with political and social meaning.[57]
From the North, realism seemed to underscore what unreconstructed Southerners had been asserting all along: an assent to
public intimacy was always more than it pretended to be.

When political claims for civil rights were apprehended as social
claims, the result was not a disappearance of the political but an
investing of personal responses and feelings with political, legal,
and scientific weight. Cable, for example, in "The Freedman's
Case in Equity," which appeared in the February 1884 *Century*,
noted that legal changes in the wake of the Civil War entailed a
"recognition of certain human rights discordant with the sentiments of those [whites] who have always called themselves the

community" and that in the South these new rights were "to be interpreted and applied under the domination of these antagonistic sentiments." As Cable described conditions in the South, African-American civil rights were subject to a judicial review based not in law but in feelings. To this situation, Cable responded by trying both to discredit the "sentiments" of reactionary white Southerners and to elevate the feelings of blacks to the status of legal "evidence." As indicated by its title, "The Freedman's Case in Equity" was meant to suggest a bill of equity, allowing Cable to take into his purview evidence that might not be relevant in other legal venues. Cable admonished his readers that "if any one can think the Freedman does not feel the indignities thus heaped upon him, let him take up any paper printed for colored men's patronage, or ask any colored man of known courageous utterance." Cable then went on to describe the "humiliation" of a genteel black woman and child whom separate car laws forced to share a railway car with "a most melancholy and revolting company" of prison inmates.[58] The point was clear. The injustice of Southern attacks on black civil rights was measured by the degree to which blacks demonstrated themselves to be, in James's words, "persons capable of feeling."[59]

Certainly, however, the door of Cable's argument could swing both ways, and the negative feelings expressed by whites when they came into social contact with blacks were also seen as substantive enough to carry legal weight.[60] When in 1903 African Americans in Montgomery, Alabama, brought a bill of equity to court in *Giles* v. *Harris* seeking "to enroll upon the voting lists the name of the plaintiff and all other qualified members of his race," Justice Oliver Wendell Holmes declared it "impossible to grant the equitable relief which is asked." Though he cited inconsistencies in the plaintiff's arguments, Holmes also held that "the court has little practical power to deal with the people of the state in a body." Although feelings per se are not mentioned in Holmes's decision, he does say that if "the great mass of the white population intends to keep the blacks from voting" then "relief . . . must be given by [whites] or by the legislative and political department of the government of the United States."[61] Black Americans seeking political redress would find themselves necessarily appealing to the feelings and sentiments of recalcitrant whites.

And as realistic novels and Jamesian representational strategies suggest, what white Americans could see was that to give an inch was to give an ell. Political and social rights were necessarily implicated.

To turn again to *The Princess Casamassima*, which was serialized in the *Atlantic Monthly*, is to find is an erosion of the supposed middle ground between politics and social feelings. If from one point of view *The Princess Casamassima* reveals, according to Mark Seltzer, the contagion of police work; from another it reveals the contagion of a democracy which does not respect the class boundaries associated with respectable marriage.[62] Through the eyes of the prince, the princess's estranged husband, and Rosy Muniment, the invalid sister of arch revolutionary Paul Muniment, politics is merely a cover for sexual liaisons. Throughout the novel Rosy Muniment insists upon reading through the motives of the upper class women who declare allegiance to the political grievances of the oppressed in order to find a romantic subtext. In regard to Lady Aurora's repeated visits to their apartment, Rosy tells her brother that Lady Aurora "'would marry you at a day's notice.'" (491). And Rosy's assessment of Lady Aurora's affection for Paul is seconded by the princess, who tells Hyacinth that Lady Aurora "'would marry her friend—your friend, Mr. Muniment.'"[63]

Matrimonial desires, however, work to make most of the central characters romantic rivals with one another. At various points in the story Hyacinth, Lady Aurora, Rosy Muniment, Paul Muniment, Captain Sholto, and Millicent Henning harbor suspicions about the romantic relations between other characters, oftentimes acting as jealous spouses or jilted lovers. When told by Madame Grandoni, the princess's aged companion, that his wife's secret meetings with men were part of a political plot, the prince replies, "'But perhaps they only pretend it's for that'" (510). And though Madame Grandoni attempts to disabuse him of that interpretation, the Prince's suspicions remain so powerful that they infect Hyacinth. As the Prince holds Hyacinth by the arm so that the two can observe the princess and Paul Muniment,

> a part of the agitation that possessed the unhappy Italian seemed to pass into [Hyacinth's] own blood; a wave of anxiety rushed through him—anxiety as to the relations of the two persons who had descended from the cab; he had, in short, for several instants, a very exact revelation of the state

of feeling of a jealous husband. If he had been told, half an hour before, that he was capable of surreptitious peepings, in the interest of such jealousy, he would have resented the insult; yet he allowed himself to be checked by his companion. (519–20)

Though Hyacinth expresses surprise at his jealousy, his feelings are not without precedent in his relations with other characters. In fact they emerge from Hyacinth's admission that he "felt at times almost as if he were married to his hostess [the princess], so many things were taken for granted between them" (482). And later, after Paul and the princess begin to spend a great deal of time together, displacing Lady Aurora and Hyacinth, respectively, the latter two come together to commiserate tacitly as ill-fated lovers who had lost "that which he or she had never had" (540).

Almost inevitably, the intimacies struck up for political reasons in *The Princess Casamassima* shade imperceptibly into romantic, erotic relationships or jealous suspicions. This shading tends to dissolve any idea of "natural" class antipathies, and permits a promiscuous dispersal of matrimonial expectations and possibilities among the various characters. Social equality becomes inseparable from demands for legal and political justice. Questions of political justice, in fact, seem to reveal themselves only through their intimate and social manifestations. Though these demands come to naught, and even end in tragedy in *The Princess Casamassima* and other realistic narratives, they become that which is thinkable in the realistic text, underscoring the immanent political threat of social intermingling. In fact, it is not quite correct to see these demands as going for naught in *The Princess Casamassima*. If Hyacinth feels like a husband towards the princess, she behaves like a wife towards him, offering to sacrifice her life in place of his and mourning by his bedside, "bending over the body while a strange low cry came from her lips" (590), following his suicide. Moreover, her liaison with Muniment does lead to a temporary redistribution of monetary capital from the upper classes to the revolutionaries. And this financial liaison forces the prince to write a letter in French to Muniment, treating as an equal a man he regards as inferior.

One must take care, however, neither to exaggerate nor to deprecate the effects of the novel as a force for political and social change. The novel was certainly accepted as a respectable genre during this period, an acceptance that embraced the writings of realists and nonrealists alike. But despite this wide acceptance, serious literature was often perceived as a potential threat to the bounds of social propriety that were being established by periodical editors. "It cannot be denied," admitted the editors of the *Century* in announcing their thirtieth semiannual volume, "that much of the world's most valuable literature, sacred and secular, could never reach the public through the pages of a 'family magazine.'" This was so, they continued, because editors were bound by "a certain unwritten guarantee that every periodical evolves from its own history and habit."[64] The derivation of a guarantee from "history and habit" suggested that a sort of common law logic underlay the principles of exclusion employed by editors of popular magazines. These principles not only determined the selection of literary texts for publication but also held sway outside the literary sphere.

For even as the editors of the *Century* were making explicit the unwritten guarantee of their editorial policy, they were taking up the question of sectional reconciliation, publishing Civil War reminiscences, debates on black civil rights, condemnations of politicians who insisted on waving the bloody shirt, and serialized novels by Twain, Howells, and James. Counseling "mutual respect, sympathy, and knowledge," the editors enjoined the South

> to put itself more and more in a position where it can observe
> facts with a calmer and deeper vision. The Northern freeman
> needs to put himself in the place of the Southern; the South-
> ern freeman in the place of the Southern *freedman*. . . . It is of
> the highest importance that the Southern majority should
> consider the opinions advanced by Mr. Cable in the name of
> the Southern minority. It is of the highest importance that
> the Northern majority should consider such a representative
> Southern statement as that of Mr. [Henry] Grady in the last
> number of the magazine.[65]

Despite the *Century*'s call for sympathy and a sharing of points of view, it did not in this debate feature the arguments of any prominent black spokespersons, and instead allowed whites to speak for African Americans. *The editors did not urge the freedman to put himself in the place of the Southern white.* Undercutting its own logic, the *Century* tacitly acknowledged that to make the same call for empathy from blacks would be to make a radical social claim. For blacks to place themselves in the place of whites would be to acknowledge the possibility of a social equality that the magazine seemed to disavow.

None of its writers spoke on behalf of social equality. The closest that any one of the participants came to making such an argument was the aforementioned Bishop Dudley's admission that he looked "for the day when race-peculiarities shall be terminated, when the unity of the race shall be manifested." But Dudley, too, covered himself by the use of temporal deferral. That day, however, "must be centuries hence. Instinct and reason, history and philosophy, science and revelation, all alike cry out against the degradation of the race by the free commingling of the tribe that is the highest with that which is lowest on the scale of development."[66]

George Washington Cable, in the same volume, found it necessary to invoke the magazine's unwritten guarantee to rebut charges that his essay "The Freedman's Case in Equity" had demanded social equality between blacks and whites. "Nothing in that paper touches or seeks to touch the domain of social privileges," he assured his readers. "The standing of the magazine in which it appears is guarantee against the possibility of the paper containing any such insult to the intelligence of enlightened society."[67] By grasping the *Century's* unwritten guarantee, Cable sought to arrest the social implications of his civil rights argument and to assure Southerners that blacks could enter society without turning it topsy-turvy.

The rapid and often violent erosion of black civil rights by the end of the decade revealed the weaknesses of such assurances. And the realistic authors who published their works in such magazines as the *Century* revealed the multifaceted role that realism played in this process, including a discrediting of sentimental reform, a willingness to concede that the spread of democracy entailed social vulgarization, and, paradoxically, a radical admission that civil and social rights were not separable but intimately related. Thus, by the end of the nineties it had become virtually impossible to advocate substantive civil rights reforms without being accused of promoting the social equality of blacks and whites which presumably would include the right of intermarriage. Civil rights would have to mean social revolution.

TWO

Aesthetics, Race, and
"Warrants of Decency"

N THE EYES of many cultural elites, literature, particularly the novel, was to be a key player in either abetting or forestalling fundamental changes to the nation's social order. Troubled by labor unrest in the North, the *Century*'s publisher, Roswell Smith, was brought to assert that the great task facing the novelist was "to postpone if not prevent the great impending struggle between labor and capital."[1] Fiction, for Smith, could buy the nation a little time during which solutions to class conflict might be found. The novels serialized in the *Century* would not only be good reading, but they would serve the social good.

By placing the novel at the center of political struggles, however, figures like Smith necessarily threw into question assumptions about literary aesthetics. Was literary value best measured by the capacity of books to move their readers to redress social wrongs or quell unrest? Or did seemingly abstract qualities like beauty deserve a place in critical judgment? Could good fiction somehow satisfy both sets of standards? The urgency of these questions was such that they were often addressed in fictional as well as in critical texts. For example, towards the end of *The Princess Casamassima*, Hyacinth Robinson, James's déclassé revolutionary protagonist reflects on the consequences of democracy:

> What was most in Hyacinth's mind was the idea, of which every pulsation of the general life of his time was a syllable, that the flood of democracy was rising over the world; that it would sweep all the traditions of the past before it; that, whatever it might fail to bring, it would at least carry in its bosom a magnificent energy; and that it might be trusted to look after its own. When democracy should have its way everywhere,

it would be its fault (whose else?) if want and suffering and crime should continue to be ingredients of the human lot. With his mixed, divided nature, his conflicting sympathies, his eternal habit of swinging from one view to another, Hyacinth regarded this prospect, in different moods, with different kinds of emotion. . . . he was afraid the democracy wouldn't care for perfect bindings or for the finest sort of conversation.[2]

The ambivalences afflicting Hyacinth center in the tensions between aesthetic and material needs. Whatever shape the seemingly ineluctable democratic order might take, its alleviation of human misery would be purchased with the finer aesthetic delights that centuries of suffering had produced. Entertaining the possibility that increasing aesthetic enjoyments might be incompatible with eradicating human suffering—that one project would entail sacrificing the other—Hyacinth articulates a troubling contingency that from time to time flitted across the consciences of many late nineteenth-century authors and reformers.

More sanguine than Hyacinth about the possibility of uniting aesthetic and material concerns was William Dean Howells. The realistic novel, at least as Howells saw it, could resolve the conflict between the aesthetic and the material. As an aestheticization of the everyday, realistic fiction could retain craft and artistry but give them new life by wedding them to the practical, the familiar, the quotidian. "Art," Howells writes in the December 1888 "Editor's Study" in *Harper's*, "is beginning to find out that if it does not make friends with Need it must perish."[3] Rather than opposing "art" to the daily concerns of ordinary people, Howells locates the very vitality of art in its responsiveness to humanity's material needs.

For a time, sharing Howells's optimism was Richard Watson Gilder, editor of *Century* magazine. Gilder had been an early promoter of Howellsian realism, publishing much of the writer's work, including Howells's notorious November 1882 review of Henry James's fiction, which declared contemporary American novels superior to most British writing of the past. In commissioning Thomas Sergeant Perry to write a critical essay on Howells in the *Century*'s first volume after the magazine had changed its name from *Scribner's*, Gilder sought to make explicit the nature of the realist aesthetic. Realism, according to Perry, was the art that mod-

ern, individualistic social relations dictated: "Struggle as we may
against it, it is one of the main conditions of American, if not of
modern, society, that inborn merit has a chance to assert itself. . . . and even if movements of this kind could be stopped, society could not revert to its original condition of rigid divisions. As
it is however, these movements are irresistible." Cloaking democracy in a mantle of inevitability, Perry pits the individual against social customs and communal mores, giving the nod to the individual, with an assist from the realistic novel. "After all," Perry writes,
"what can realism produce but the downfall of conventionality?
Just as the scientific spirit digs the ground from beneath supersti-
tion, so does its fellow-worker, realism, tend to prick the bubble of
abstract types. Realism is the tool of the democratic spirit, the modern spirit by which the truth is elicited."[4]

Viewed in this light, realism and the magazines that early on
championed the writers associated with that literary movement—
Howells, James, and Mark Twain—would presumably have proved
a formidable ally in the quest for black political equality, providing
another weapon for puncturing the armor of conventions and mores that defined interracial relations in post–Civil War America.
George Washington Cable certainly thought so when he told the
1883 graduating class of Louisiana State University that literature
"must be free . . . to rectify thoughts, morals, manners, society,
even though it shake the established order of things like an earth-
quake."[5] And Gilder's decision to publish Cable's work in the *Century*, particularly his essay "The Freedman's Case in Equity," which
broadly championed the racial integration of schools and other
public places, would indicate some meeting of the minds on this
question. This conflation of aesthetics and politics suggested that
as realism secured a position as the dominant aesthetic in the nation's most prestigious magazines the unfinished business of black
political liberation would emerge from the relative oblivion that
had enveloped it following the abandonment of Radical Reconstruction and return to a central place in the national agenda.

This dual promise was not to be fulfilled. Though realism and
race relations were hotly debated during these years—the latter
more so in the early part of that decade—the political fortunes of
black Americans ebbed to the nadir of the 1890s and realists saw
their aesthetic hopes put on hold for a later generation of writers.
The genteel magazines like the *Century*, which represented them-

selves as vehicles for progressive change supporting such causes as civil service reform and an international copyright law, also played a role in these failures. As noted by C. Vann Woodward, "It was quite common in the 'eighties and 'nineties to find in the *Nation*, *Harper's Weekly*, the *North American Review*, or the *Atlantic Monthly* Northern liberals and former abolitionists mouthing the shibboleths of white supremacy regarding the Negro's innate inferiority, shiftlessness, and hopeless unfitness for full participation in the white man's civilization."[6] And as we saw in the previous chapter, the *Century* readily admitted that its editorial policies precluded the publication of a great deal of excellent and important fiction. Customs and communal mores were not, after all, to be committed to the rubbish heap.

My interest here, however, is not only the political conservatism of magazines like the *Century* in regard to race and aesthetics but the degree to which writers who saw themselves as challenging the status quo depended on, and even supported, the "decency" of the monthlies in an effort to clothe the potential radicalism of their enterprises in the commonplace, noncontroversial garb of the everyday. Realism need not require immorality or gratuitous muckraking. In the words of Perry, Howells "has proved that realism does not mean groping in the mire,"[7] and that a considerable social distance could separate the realist and the muckraking journalist. Neither did supporting black political equality require advocating racial social equality. When his publications in *Century*, particularly "The Freedman's Case in Equity," were charged with being arguments for the social equality of the races, Cable, as we have seen, cited the magazine's reputation in his defense.[8]

The unimpeachable moral standing of Northern monthlies was something on which these writers counted. For Howells, the *Century*'s willingness to publish a novel like *A Modern Instance*, in which he takes up the controversial issue of divorce, was crucial. The magazine provided the author a measure of protection against critics who would charge him with immorality. And when such charges came, the *Century* was ready with a defense, opining that "we are inclined to believe that since *Uncle Tom's Cabin* there has appeared no American work of fiction having a stronger and wider moral bearing, or of greater power to affect public sentiment."[9] Correspondingly, Cable found that Gilder's perceived sympathy for Southern authors and his willingness to criticize those Republicans

who insisted on "waving the bloody shirt" was potentially a plus for
a liberal who wanted his thoughts represented not as radicalism
but as true Southern opinion that had been suppressed or per-
verted by a vocal but unrepresentative majority.

Also in Cable's favor was a point made by Woodward: the active
involvement of American monthly magazines in suturing the
wounds that disfigured postbellum society. The Civil War, the as-
sassination of one president, the impeachment of another, Reconstruction, election scandals, and increased immigration had created a nation that was hungry for legitimate consensus. By the
1880s Gilder was openly enlisting his magazine in the cause of sectional reconciliation. Under his guidance the magazine had com-
missioned a series of Civil War reminiscences which ran from November 1884 through November 1887 and a biography of
Abraham Lincoln. The point of the Civil War project, according to
Gilder, was "the 'unveiling of all hearts.' If the North can see the
heart of the South, and the South the North's, they will love each
other as never before! This is truth, and not sentimentalism."[10]
Similarly, the *Century*'s "Life of Lincoln" was to "have a great moral
and political effect in that it will help to unite the North and South
as never before, around the story and experiences of the great
President."[11]

Gilder's belief that work of reconciliation was yet to be completed by 1880 highlights the ambivalent stance that Northern periodicals and magazines had adopted at the close of the war, attempting to claim an ideological victory even as they argued the
need for continued agitation on behalf of the freedmen. While the
civil rights agenda seemed secure—"Nobody," *The Nation* proclaimed in 1865, "whose opinion is of any consequence, maintains
any longer that [blacks'] claim to political equality is not a sound
one"—*The Nation* also warned against complacency. The Southern
ruling class was still recalcitrant, and the bulk of the freedmen
were uneducated and untrained. The writer, therefore, cautioned
that "freedom bestowed on a man left in the position in which we
have placed the freedman, only increases the number of points at
which he can be assailed and tormented."[12] The tightrope that *The
Nation* sought to walk was ostensibly the path from a slave to a free
society. And *The Nation*'s article tried to represent the slender
thread of African-American political equality as a broad highway,
beset only by lawless bands of highwaymen. But as the 1860s gave

way to the 1870s, among those highwaymen were not only recalcitrant Southerners but hotheaded Northerners who continued to
insist that the power of the state should be used on behalf of the
beleaguered freedmen.[13]

By the 1880s drawing distinctions between, on the one hand, realistic aesthetics and the call for black political rights and, on the
other, "truly" subversive political activity was an attempt to locate
realism and black political struggle within a domain of order that
could reestablish national unity. As Gilder acknowledged, realistic
fiction did on occasion push the limits of social propriety, but even
when it did so, he was quick to assure his subscribers, the net effect
of these texts was to support social order. Responding to a reader
who thought Mark Twain too vulgar a writer to appear in *Century*,
Gilder admitted that Twain was "at times . . . inartistically and in-
defensibly coarse," and that "there is much of his writing that we
would not print for a miscellaneous audience," but he went on to
defend Twain as "a good citizen . . . [who] believes in the best
things."[14] Gilder also noted that Twain had given "his full consent"
to Gilder's editing of excerpts from *Huckleberry Finn*. Certainly, the
mere fact that Twain had to be edited indicated that the marriage
of realism and propriety was a rocky one; but the partners had not
been deemed fully incompatible.

Related to this question of propriety was whether any literary aesthetic could secure itself to the social and political needs of the African American and still remain recognizable as an aesthetic. Gilder's initial support of Cable suggests that during the early 1880s
he felt that the answer to such a question was "Yes." Collaborating
assiduously with Cable during the composition of *Dr. Sevier*, which
the magazine serialized in 1883, Gilder complained to Cable that
in the early drafts "you have turned your mind so completely into
philanthropical work that for the time being you have lost your
sense of art. I do not object to philanthropy either in life and act,
nor in a book—but its expression must, in a work of art, take an artistic form. You and I do not object to the morality and spiritual
teaching of Hawthorne, nor to the patriotism and philanthropy of
Tourgueneff (whose writings, it is said, freed the Russian serfs) because the form is always artistic."[15] Art and political efficacy could
be reconciled provided the artistic agenda was kept center stage.
This belief guided Gilder's editing of Cable, and after a series of exchanges and revisions the novel was accepted for publication. But

Cable's insistence in subsequent work on foregrounding the political message of his literary endeavors proved a continual difficulty for the editor of the *Century*, and by the end of the decade, disappointed with the manuscript for Cable's *John March, Southerner*, Gilder lamented to the author that the novel represented "instead of a return *to* literature, an attempt to fetch everything into literature save & except literature itself. . . . Shades of Tourgée!" He then warned Cable to "remember the fate of Tolstoi."[16]

In linking Cable with Albion Tourgée, Gilder was speaking unequivocally. Tourgée's *A Fool's Errand* (1879), which had combined an account of the Reconstruction period with a love story, suggested that a dose of political realism and fictional sentimental romance might successfully reawaken the nation's passions on behalf of justice for the freedmen. Tourgée's novel criticized openly the North's lack of resolve in pushing forward a successful Reconstruction program, called upon "the Nation [to] educate the colored man and the poor-white man *because* the Nation held them in bondage, and is responsible for their education," and presented an almost documentary account of the rise of the Ku Klux Klan. The novel was instantly a bestseller and was compared to *Uncle Tom's Cabin*. Most provocatively, the novel advocated the use of Northern military force to secure and safeguard the civil rights of black Americans while making central the extent to which this enterprise had forever changed the nation's construction of liberal democracy. According to Tourgée's novel, what many Northerners had failed to see was that "the North is simply a conqueror; and, if the results she fought for are to be secured, she must rule as a conqueror." And though this failure of vision doomed Reconstruction, the changes wrought in the nation's vision of democracy were such that at the very least the Reconstruction experiment had "formulated a confession of error. It gave us a construction of 'we the people' in the preamble of our Federal Constitution which gave the lie to that which had formally prevailed."[17]

As successful as Tourgée was with *A Fool's Errand*, his subsequent fictions failed to impress his readers with the urgency of his political message. In Gilder's opinion the reasons for this failure were not far to seek. Tourgée's novels were little more than political tracts. There was, however, no guarantee that had Cable expressed his opinions in an essay rather than a novel they would have passed muster with Gilder. The magazine's limits were ideological as well as aesthetic. Although the *Century* had backed Cable during the controversy generated by the publication of "The Freedman's Case in Equity" and "The Silent South," Gilder took a different position when Cable recommended that the *Century* publish an essay by Charles Chesnutt on the race question, saying that "Mr. Chesnutt's paper—'The Negro's Answer to the Negro Question,' is a timely political paper. So timely and *so* political—in fact so partisan—that we cannot handle it. It should appear at once somewhere."[18] Somewhere, however, was clearly not the *Century*. Gilder's magazine was also not the place for Cable's *John March, Southerner*, which eventually saw publication in *Scribner's*.

Avoiding the appearance of partisanship and extremism was a price Gilder was willing to pay in order to secure and maintain the *Century*'s position as the nation's preeminent monthly. It was also a strategy employed by progressive reformers. From the end of the Civil War into the 1890s, political and literary authors of radical bent often adopted a posture of articulating a commonsense, widely shared point of view that stood in opposition to, or had been cowed into silence by, subversive ideas, uncontrolled passions, misunderstandings, and bad habits. African-American activist and novelist Frances E. W. Harper sought to assure white audiences that black Americans were not of the revolutionary element that was threatening the nation. In an article entitled "Duty to Dependent Races," she proclaimed that "today the hands of the negro are not dripping with dynamite. We do not read of his flaunting the red banners of anarchy in the face of the nation, nor plotting in beer saloons to overthrow existing institutions, nor spitting on the American flag."[19] The anarchist underworld of London that James had sketched in *The Princes Casamassima* was not the world of the black American. And if Howells had to be asked by Gilder to remove the word "dynamite" from the April installment of *Silas Lapham* in the *Century* (because "it is an unknown and horribly inflammable quantity, and we don't want, if we can help it, to be associated with the subject, except in opposing it",)[20] black Americans needed no such reminders.

At best these efforts provided a small amount of breathing space in which potentially radical ideas could put in a claim for the mantle of respectability. At worst such tactics created or exacerbated destructive schisms among progressive communities as when white suffragist leaders like Susan B. Anthony and Elizabeth Cady Stanton sought alliances with Southern reactionaries against the ratification of the Fifteenth Amendment because it extended the vote to black men before white women.[21]

Cable's concept of the silent South, which provided the title for his September 1885 *Century* essay, was another such attempt having ambiguous results. The idea of a silent South, composed of "the best men of the South [who] are coming daily into convictions that condemn their own beliefs of yesterday as the antiquated artillery of an outgrown past,"[22] was an attempt to assure Southern readers that Cable, a Southerner by birth who had fought for the Confederacy, was not out of step with the feelings and temperaments of his native region. Having gained celebrity through publication in a Northern journal and having moved North for his wife's health and for financial reasons, Cable was vulnerable to charges of having betrayed his region and of becoming an outsider to those for whom he claimed to be a spokesman. The silent South, of which Cable did see some evidence, was a way of putting forth his positions not as Northern but as Southern through and through. According to Cable, he was not alone in abhorring the "semi-slavery" of Jim Crow, "for there are thousands of Southern-born white men and women, in the minority in all places—in churches, courts, schools, libraries, theaters, concert halls, and on steamers and railway carriages—who see the wrong and folly of these things, silently blush for them, and withhold their open protest only because their belief is unfortunately stronger in the futility of their counsel than in the power of a just cause." Cable concluded this observation by saying, "I do not justify their silence; But I affirm their sincerity and their goodly numbers."[23]

Cable's faith, however, was not rewarded. Southern voices of support for black civil rights failed to provide the chorus of opinion that Cable anticipated. And as well shall see presently, one of the voices raised in response was not one that could help him much. The liberal Southerner found himself reviled as an apostate to the norms of decent society.

For realists the continued popularity of rival genres suggested that the ideology of realism, like that of racial equality, was not borne upon the mainstream of American literary tastes. Yet in 1887, when responding to the charge that American readers would not support the sort of literary masterpieces he was championing, Howells proclaimed his faith in "the power of the ordinary mind to appreciate the best. Much of the best," he continued "fails of due recognition, but enough of the best gets through to make us hopeful that when literature comes close to life, even ordinary minds will feel and know its charm." For support of his position he pointed to the popularity of Mark Twain whose works were "masterpieces of humor."[24] Like Cable, Howells identified a usually silent constituency who would readily respond when the proper notes were struck. And like Cable, Howells was to be disappointed.

For example, a great deal of negative criticism greeted the publication of Howells's *The Minister's Charge* (1886), a novel which, though focusing on genteel characters, offered a brief portrayal of petty criminals and life inside a jail. The public outcry led Howells to write to James that

> in many quarters here the book meets with little but misconception. If we regard it as nothing but an example of work in the new way—the performance of a man who won't and can't keep on doing what's been done already—its reception here by most of the reviewers is extremely discouraging. Of all grounds in the world they take the genteel ground, and every "Half bred rogue that groomed his mother's cow," reproaches me for introducing him to low company. This has been the tone of "society" about it; in the newspapers it hardly stops short of personal defamation. Of course they entirely miss the very simple purpose of the book. Nevertheless it sells, and sells bravely, and to my surprise I find myself not really caring a great deal for the printed animosity, except as it means ignorance. I suspect it's an effect of the frankness about our civilization which you have sometimes wondered I could practice with impunity. The impunity's gone, now, I assure you.[25]

The critics failed to render a just appreciation of Howells's efforts because the book seemed to drag them into the mire. The protection that serialization in a monthly should have accorded Howells does not shield him from personal defamation. He can no longer offer his criticisms with impunity.

And yet the book sells. This fact seems to provide Howells evidence that the larger public did appreciate his novel despite the "genteel" demurrals. Yet even in this respect Howells could not take too much comfort. For despite his belief that public taste could recognize "the best," Howells had indicated elsewhere that this taste was suspect. Best-sellers were often works that Howells deemed to be of dubious moral value. In a revealing "Editor's Study" column in *Harper's,* Howells relates an autobiographical episode in which he attempts to purchase for a "young lady" a novel from a newsstand at a train station. Finding that the covers and contents of these popular novels displayed "upon the whole rather more kissing and embracing going on in colors than was quite in taste" Howells instead "bought several magazines, of the kind whose name is an absolute warrant of decency, to say the least." But Howells's retreat to the safety of the editorial guarantees of propriety could serve only as a partial refuge because of his own commitment to "serious" fiction. Elsewhere in the "Editor's Study," for example, Howells had maintained that even good literature often catered to the prurient side of public tastes. And in supporting the enactment of an international copyright law that would free authors from the moral strictures of monthly magazines by making it profitable to publish a novel without first having it serialized, Howells grants novelists a license to explore such topics as "guilty love" while enjoying "the absolute artistic freedom of Tolstoi and Flaubert."[26] Carried to its logical culmination, this aspect of Howells's positions on realism, copyright, and artistic freedom put him at odds with the editorial standards of the major monthly magazines. Were Howells's work to approach the honesty of the European novelist, it, too, would find no place as a serial, as the critics of *The Minister's Charge* were not at all reluctant to point out.

What the invocation of social propriety on the part of Howells's critics seemed to make clear was that such norms would have to be challenged if realistic aesthetics were to prevail. But here Howells was at an impasse. Realism was not the only literary mode to challenge genteel norms; popular literature did so as well—and not in the name of higher literary standards but solely, in his judgment, for the purpose of achieving popularity. If it were to succeed without pandering to popular tastes, realism would have to work out some sort of compromise with gentility: it would have to "deal with Tolstoi's and Flaubert's subjects . . . in the manner of George Eliot, of Thackery, of Dickens, of society."[27]

Howells's willingness to compromise rather than reject the aesthetic demands of "society" was not merely a matter of expediency but also a matter political efficacy. Coupled with literary questions was his belief that a commitment to social propriety also provided a sure path to democratic values. Writing in the 1895 *Century* under the title "Equality as the Basis of Good Society," which might have been interpreted as a call for radical change, Howells reassured the magazine's readers that he was only observing what was already the case: polite society was "an image of a righteous state on earth."[28]

Maintaining this identity of righteousness and good society, however, had been tricky. "Society" could behave oppressively and irrationally. When Bromfield Corey opined in a draft of the April installment of Howells's *The Rise of Silas Lapham* that "in some of my walks on the Hill and down on the Back Bay, nothing but the surveillance of the local policeman prevents me from applying dynamite to those long rows of close-shuttered, handsome, brutally insensible houses,"[29] Gilder had responded with alarm, warning that "it is the very word, *dynamite,* that is now so dangerous, for any of us to use, except in condemnation."[30] Despite the fact that the novel qualifies its revolutionary sentiments by having other characters reassure the *Century*'s readers "that generally a poor man was satisfied if he could make both ends meet" and that "it's the fellows from countries where they've been kept from thinking about it [revolution] that are discontented,"[31] Gilder maintained his objection to the word and Howells complied by substituting "offering personal violence" for "applying dynamite."[32]

Gilder feared that Howells's words might link the writer too closely with "the crank who does the deed."[33] And when a bomb exploded at an anarchists' rally at Haymarket Square in Chicago on the fourth of May 1886, killing policeman Mathias Degan, Gilder seemed prescient in seeing the possibility of violence and Howells's connection to it. The nation reacted hysterically to the incident, and eight known anarchists—August Spies, Albert Parsons, Louis Lingg, Machael Schwab, Samuel Fielden, George Engel, Adolph Fischer, and Oscar Neebe—none of whom were identified by witnesses, were convicted of murder "on the grounds that they had resorted to incendiary and seditious language on numerous occasions, and that by preaching hatred of policemen, Pinkerton agents, and other law-enforcement officials they had in effect caused the death of Mathias Degan."[34] Seven of the men, four of whom were eventually hanged, received death sentences; one was

sentenced to fifteen years imprisonment. Of the three others sentenced to death, one committed suicide and the other two had
their sentences commuted to life imprisonment.

Howells protested the sentences vigorously. He petitioned the
governor of Illinois to have all the sentences commuted, and he
wrote a letter to the *New York Tribune* urging others to support him.
As far as drumming up support was concerned, Howells's appeal
fell on deaf ears, and for his pains he was ridiculed and roundly
condemned. In assessing the implications of the Haymarket verdict, Howells saw it as a fundamental assault on political dissent. In
a second, unmailed letter to the *Tribune* dated 12 November 1887,
he wrote:

> We had a political execution in Chicago yesterday. The
> sooner we realize this, the better for us. By such a perversion
> of law as brought the Anarchists to their doom, William Lloyd
> Garrison, who published a paper denouncing the constitu
> tion as a compact with hell and a covenant with death, and
> every week stirred up the blacks and their friends throughout
> the country to abhor the social system of the South, could
> have been sent to the gallows if a slave had killed his masters.
> Emerson, Parker, and Howe, Giddings and Wade, Sumner
> and Greeley, and all who encouraged the war against slavery
> in Kansas, and the New England philanthropists who sup
> plied the Free State men with Sharp's rifles could have been
> held "morally responsible," and made to pay with their per
> sons, when John Brown took seven Missourians out of their
> beds and shot them. Wendell Phillips, and Thoreau, and the
> other literary men whose sympathy inflamed Brown to homi
> cidal insurrection at Harper's Ferry, could have been put to
> death with the same justice that consigned the Anarchists to
> the gallows in Chicago.[35]

In Howells's view, the political climate of the 1880s was such that it
would have imperiled the tradition of New England dissent that
had been greatly responsible for the abolition of slavery. Further,
had Howells insisted on using the word *dynamite* in *Silas Lapham*,
the logic of the Haymarket verdict would have at some level implicated him as well. Given the willingness of the empowered classes
to disregard principle in suppressing perceived threats to social order, the very language of dissent was by implication legally action-

able. This is not to say that Howells's novels had necessarily brought him within the purview of the police power of the state. The public censure he occasionally fell victim to never found its way into a magistrate's writ. It is the case, however, that such a possibility was certainly on the minds of the editor and publisher of the *Century* when they asked Howells to change the wording of the passage from *Silas Lapham*. In justifying the *Century*'s intrusion on the text, Roswell Smith wrote Howells saying, "I fancy the Law might stop the Magazine or make the Publisher trouble in England."[36] At the very least, the language of equality had become recognizable only as social subversion, and after reading Howells's *Annie Kilburn*, former president Rutherford Hayes observed that in American public debate "I do not find a ready word for the doctrine of true equality of rights. Its foes call it nihilism, communism, socialism, and the like. Howells would perhaps call it justice."[37]

Given the prevailing political winds and the testiness of editors and publishers like Gilder and Smith, Howells's support of "justice" clearly required compromises. The problem he faced was whether any compromise could be made without giving away the store. Good society certainly found it difficult to embrace anarchism. No less a New England fixture than Julia Ward Howe, the abolitionist who penned "The Battle Hymn of the Republic," negatively assessed the Haymarket anarchists in an essay entitled "Is Polite Society Polite?" Howe averred that "in order to be polite, it is important to cultivate polite ways of thinking. Great social troubles and even crimes grow out of rude and selfish habits of mind. Let us take the case of the Anarchists who were executed in Chicago some years ago. Before their actions became wicked, their thoughts became very impolite." As a virtue, politeness in Howe's essay became indistinguishable from deference to the "laws [that] compel the capitalist to make roads for the use of the poor man, and to build schoolhouses for the education of his children."[38] Any further demands, any challenge to the law and to capital as such became potentially impolite and ultimately wicked.

But Howe's own abolitionist heritage was vulnerable to the change of having been impolite. As realist novels attempted to represent the abolitionist past, politeness, taste, and legitimacy seemed to drain away even from that legacy: Silas Lapham's parlor decor, which includes "a marble group of several figures, expressing an Italian conception of Lincoln Freeing the Slaves,—a Latin

negro and his wife,—with an Eagle flapping his wings in approval,
at Lincoln's feet," is emblematic of the family's poor artistic taste.[39]
The feminist reformers in James's *The Bostonians,* who trace their
ideological lineages back to old abolitionists and who seek to keep
alive that self-denying spirit of sacrifice, are presented as emotion-
ally disfigured, politically inept, and sexually disturbed vestiges of
a bygone age. And Huck Finn finds his eloquent and morally heroic decision to rescue Jim rendered superfluous by a narrative
trick which has made Jim an already free man.

How thoroughly the reformist spirit threatened to be exiled
from the aesthetic of the "common" might be measured by the
tone and content of Howells's comments in 1886 when he had occasion to review Sarah Bradford's biographical sketch of Harriet
Tubman. The review, brief as it is, includes much praise and admiration for Tubman, yet it is an admiration that has to struggle in
order to conjure up the reality of its object. Tubman's heroic actions strike Howells as "nothing within the date of actual history. . . . We can hardly imagine such things now for the purposes
of fiction; all troubles that now hurt and threaten us are as crumpled rose leaves in our couch."

Appearing in the same column in which Howells makes the infamous invitation to "our novelists, therefore, to concern themselves with the more smiling aspects of life, which are the more
American, and to seek the universal in the individual rather than
the social interests,"[40] Howells's remarks on Tubman signal how
difficult it would be to reconcile African-American political needs
with the art of the real. Having been dismissed aesthetically as a de-
ficiency in taste, equal rights claims could also become assaults on
the genteel norms that, according to Cable, no one of proper
breeding—white or black—would want circumvented. When, in *A
Modern Instance,* an upstanding newspaper editor named Ricker
complains about the rise of sensationalistic journalism, he does so
in a way that gives a vulgar cast to what ought to be a demand for
justice. "I have doubted a good while," he opines,

> whether a drunken Irishman who breaks his wife's head, or a
> child who falls into a tub of hot water, has really established a
> claim on the public interest. Why should I be told by tele-
> graph how three negroes died on the gallows in North Caro-
> lina? Why should an accurate correspondent inform me of

the elopement of a married man with his maidservant in East Machias? Why should I sup on all the horrors of a railroad accident, and have the bleeding fragments hashed up for me at breakfast?[41]

Lynching, violence against women, child neglect, adultery, and railroad accidents all become indistinguishable intrusions at the middle-class breakfast table. To be sure, underwriting Ricker's complaint against yellow journalism is the role that the print media played in stirring up public passion against blacks and creating a hunger for sensation that could sate itself only in mob action. "Mob spirit," observed Ida B. Wells "is encouraged by the 'leading citizens' and the press."[42] In fact, so heinous was the role of the press in fomenting lawlessness that William James counseled in 1903 that the "epidemic of lynching" might most readily be cured "by stopping the publication of reports of lynchings" because "the social retrogression which we are witnessing is being hurried on by what is known as yellow journalism."[43] Neither Wells nor James suggested ignoring the problem, each calling for immediate and resolute action. On the other hand, though, Ricker's reactions in the passage above provide no means of responding to the sensationalized reports of misery and injustice other than as objects of disgust. The plight of women, of poor Irish, and of African Americans as victims of social injustice are represented as vulgar demands for social intimacy, suggesting that the restoration of decorum and order will potentially, if not inevitably, involve a reconstruction of social distance between black and white persons in American society.

Although Howells's image of contemporary troubles as crumpled rose leaves in a couch was meant to deprecate the social and political troubles of the 1880s, it also inadvertently underscored the political explosiveness of these same issues. Signifying romance, domesticity, and intimacy, the image implied that all social problems were related to, if not centered in, genteel households, and could emerge only in terms of their relationship to these households. For example, towards the end of Howells's critically maligned *The Minister's Charge,* which ran in the *Century* from February through December 1886, a central character, the Reverend Sewell, delivers a sermon on "complicity" in which he asserts that "no one for good or for evil, for sorrow or joy, for sickness or health, stood apart from his fellows, but each was bound to the highest and the lowest by ties that centered in the hand of God. . . . If a community was corrupt, if an age was immoral, it was not because of the vicious, but the virtuous who fancied themselves indifferent spectators."[44] Pricking the complacent consciences of his middle-class congregation, Sewell's sermon is interpreted as referring to the failure of the telegraph workers strike. But Sewell is pointing in a more general direction. As the events of the novel illustrate, the actions of individual characters, including Sewell himself, end up contributing to the troubles of Lemuel Barker, the country boy who becomes the minister's "charge," and who, as result of the actions of others, comes to know poverty, crime, shame, and guilt. Interpersonal relations in this novel are not merely representations but are constitutive of the social whole. The less fortunate had legitimate social claims upon the households of the more fortunate.

But the lesson of Haymarket in 1887 seemed to impress upon Howells the impotence of middle-class radicalism. The reality of middle-class life was its inability to get beyond its own circle of existence. Howells's *April Hopes* (1888), which he called his first novel "written with the distinct consciousness that he was writing as a realist,"[45] suggests that Howells became intent on limiting realism to the rather banal vicissitudes of daily life, the whole novel revolving around the on-again, off-again courtship of his central characters. Even the sensationalistic newspaper *The Events,* which in *A Modern Instance* is represented as one of the forces of social disorder, becomes in *April Hopes* the voice of common sense through the wry observations of a young man named Boardman.

In the wake of this change, Sewell's sermon on complicity gives way to the silly and self-centered efforts of many of Howells's 1880s upper- and middle-class characters who play at philanthropy and end up inflicting more harm than good on their victim-charges. As Howells had grown at once impressed and depressed by the example of Tolstoy's renunciation of privilege and claim to have thrown in his lot with the poor, the American realist simultaneously honored and ridiculed the attempts of his characters to do likewise. His 1888 novel, *Annie Kilburn,* exposes the hypocrisy of American aristocrats who merely condescend to the working classes in attempting to establish a social union. The novel, however, also kills off the idealistic Reverend Peck before he can make good his attempt to go and work among the working class, his death driving home the difficulty of successful philanthropy by the privileged classes. The Reverend Peck's tragedy seems to leave Howells's middle-class reader with the following lesson: "'We people of leisure, or comparative leisure, have really nothing in common with you people who work with your hands for a living; and as we really can't be friends with you, we won't patronise you. We won't advise you, and we won't help you; but here's the money. If you fail, you fail; and if you succeed, you won't succeed by our aid and comfort.'"[46]

Howells's hardnosed look at class antagonisms in *Annie Kilburn* and the emphasis on the importance of economic control was perhaps a step forward. However, in a climate where the nation as a whole was willing to declare the lower classes as a hostile Other and to seek means of avoiding its responsibilities to these groups, Howells's realism may have had an effect less helpful than he had hoped. The "needs" of the lower classes, when represented through genteel spokesmen, emerged as grotesque rather than artistic.

Despite Howells's claims to the contrary, the realistic novel worked toward a new definition of narrative genre in part by defining an aesthetic that acknowledged its inability to represent the needs of oppressed and debased peoples on the American scene, particularly African Americans. When Howells, in *An Imperative Duty* (1891), turned directly to the fictional representation of the problem of race, his narrative resolution pointed to the incompatibility of generic definition and the demands of social uplift. Upon discovering that she is of part black ancestry, the novel's heroine, Rhoda Aldgate, tells her white suitor, a Dr. Olney, that duty compels her to refuse his offer of marriage and go South to serve the race: "Oughtn't I to go down there and help them; try to educate them, and elevate them; give my life to them? Isn't it base and cowardly to desert them, and live happily apart from them?" Olney responds quite logically that inasmuch as she hasn't lived with her black relatives and is of only one-sixteenth black ancestry, that she owes more to the white race than she does to the black: "Begin with *me*," he says. "You won't find me unreasonable. All that I shall ask of you are the fifteen-sixteenths or so of you that belong to my race by heredity; and I will cheerfully consent to your giving our colored connections their one-sixteenth."[47] Clearly, within the context of the novel, Olney's response is the correct one. It properly explodes the fiction of race identity and the "one drop" belief. It also accords with the novel's characterization of Rhoda, who views blacks as alternately exotic and grotesque and would be ill-equipped to engage in her projected agenda of racial uplift without insufferable condescension.

On the other hand, Olney's commonsense response to Rhoda's proposed sacrifice quietly slides questions of black education into the container of romanticized duties that Howells satirizes again and again in his work. To be sure, Howells's commitment on matters of race was genuine. He was a founding member of the NAACP. Additionally, W. E. B. Du Bois lauded *An Imperative Duty* as having "faced our national foolishness and shuffling and evasion."[48] But in contrast to *Silas Lapham,* in which Silas's moral decision requires that he give weight to the interests of a community to which he has no visible ties, *An Imperative Duty* presents a muddier picture of morality, duty, and the legitimate claims of community. In *An Imperative Duty,* a decision to serve the needs of unseen black Southerners is represented as so much romantic nonsense. Although "Art," in Howells's view, ought to make friends with "Need," the need of realism to distinguish itself from competing genres and literary conventions and to remain distinguishable from a purely philanthropic enterprise created a number of potential conflicts.

An Imperative Duty, for example, seemed to oppose the political and aesthetic positions taken by black women during the 1890s. While Howells's novel parodied the sentimentalized, self-sacrifice of the tragic mulatta figure that had already become a commonplace in American fiction, his critique also drew into its orbit the belief that black women could and should play a role in combating racist oppression in a public way. Over the long term, Claudia Tate has argued, the "critical evaluations that privilege realistic depictions of the so-called race problem have been largely responsible for the low esteem that traditional Afro-American scholarship has routinely accorded nineteenth-century black women's sentimental narratives."[49] And, it is only recently that critics have acknowledged how the voices raised by black women sound a note "that surely devastates William Dean Howells's *An Imperative Duty* for that novel's myopic assumption that a polite mulatto woman would find no suitable companionship among any given assembly of black people."[50]

Frances Harper's *Iola Leroy, or Shadows Uplifted,* which also appeared in book form in 1892, takes a position almost diametrically opposed to Howells's. In her story, Iola, the fair-skinned black heroine who only belatedly discovers the "truth" of her identity, refuses the marriage proposal of Dr. Gresham, a white physician, asserting a kinship with her recently acknowledged race. Gresham, like Howells's Dr. Olney, urges the woman he loves to be reasonable about her racial obligation, telling Iola, "if you love your race, as you call it, work for it, suffer for it, and, if need be, die for it; but don't marry it." Iola, however, is not as easily dissuaded as Rhoda, insisting on her indebtedness to her darker brothers and sisters: "It was . . . through their unrequited toil that I was educated, while they were compelled to live in ignorance. I am indebted to them for the power I have to serve them."[51] Iola also has what Rhoda lacks—an alternative suitor (in the person of Dr. Latimer) who is black, educated, and fair-skinned.

With these differences in place, the sentiments that appear humorous and slightly ridiculous in Howells's novel emerge not only as reasonable but as heroic in Harper's romance. Meanwhile Howells's solution becomes politically suspect. The offer of "love, home, and social position" from Dr. Gresham, which mirrors Olney's proposal to Rhoda, is treated by Harper as a bribe to commit treason to the race.[52] Inasmuch as "Harper's novel was as much a part of [her] political program of uplift as her lectures and activism,"[53] Howells's narrative critique of novels of sentimental duty in *An Imperative Duty* carries an ominous weight. His commonsense position apparently denied the legitimacy of the very public forum that women like Harper sought to occupy and the vocational choices they sought to endorse.

In support of Harper was Anna Julia Cooper's *A Voice from the South,* which was presented as an answer to Cable's plea that the "Silent South" abandon its reticence and give voice to its true sentiments on behalf of racial justice. Cable, of course, was listening primarily for the assent of white Southerners to his views. Black voices, he assumed, had already spoken. But Cooper's text was a pointed reminder that "one important witness has not yet been heard from. . . . the Black Woman." And *A Voice* is an eloquent plea that true democracy requires the active participation of black women. Cooper's censures on various writers were severe. She said that on the race question "Mr. Howells does not know what he is talking about." Censuring the realist for his "misrepresentations," Cooper worried that *An Imperative Duty,* like the Columbian Exposition in Chicago, created the impression that African Americans were only "bootblacks and hotel waiters, grinning from ear to ear and bowing and courtesying for the extra tips."[54]

However, the opposition between Howells and Cooper and Harper was not as stark as Cooper maintains. In *An Imperative Duty* black woman achieve public presence and legitimacy—contributing to the "vividness of the public spectacle"—by creating "an effect both of gentleness and gentility" that contrasted with the behavior of the other ethnics in Boston's emerging proletariat.[55] African Americans in Howells's novel represent not a threat to genteel order but a "natural" conduit for the transmission of genteel values. Likewise, Harper's novel was committed to the political power of black gentility as embodied in her central characters. And one of the axes that Cooper grinds in her critique of *An Imperative Duty* is not Howells's stress on gentility but his failure to generalize it to an entire class of African Americans. "Howells," she laments,

> has met colored persons in hotels or on the commons promenading and sparking, or else acting as menials and lazzaroni.
> He has not seen, and therefore cannot be convinced, that there exists a quiet, self-respecting, dignified class of easy life and manners (save only where it crosses the roughness of their white fellow countrymen's barbarity) of cultivated tastes and habits, and with no more in common with the class of his acquaintance than the accident of complexion.[56]

What Howells presented as a racial trait, Cooper defined as a class difference within races. In a real way, however, the two were largely in agreement. The nation could find an otherwise vanishing gentility if it considered its black citizens. And but for "sympathy" or "duty," the attitude of "well-bred" blacks towards laborers in Cooper's estimation was the same as the attitude that genteel whites felt for the laborer in Howells's *Annie Kilburn.*

Also, neither Harper nor Cooper could escape drawing invidious distinctions between Southern black laborers and Northern immigrant workers. In some respects, both writers echo Olney's observations that black workers offer significant advantages. Harper's characterization of black Americans as a nonsubversive, non-revolutionary force in her essay "Duty to Dependent Races" is revoiced in her novel almost verbatim by Dr. Latimer.[57] And Cooper proclaimed in *A Voice from the South* that America needs the Negro for ballast if for nothing else [because] his instinct for law and order, his inborn respect for authority, his inaptitude for rioting and anarchy, his gentleness and cheerfulness as a laborer, and his deep-rooted faith in God will prove indispensable and invaluable elements in a nation menaced as America is by anarchy, socialism, communism, and skepticism poured in with all the jail birds from the continents of Europe and Asia.

Whatever black Americans were, they were not threats to the social order that Victorian American society held dear. To be sure, the animus toward immigrant workers stemmed from an awareness of the racial prejudice prevailing among supposedly radical labor unions in the North. In explaining why she found "it impossible to catch the fire of sympathy and enthusiasm for most of these labor movements at the North," Cooper cited the discrimination that blacks experienced at the hands of "amalgamated associations and labor unions of immigrant laborers." In many respects, however, what was at issue for Cooper was not so much the fact that racism prevented the alliance of white and black laborers. As a staunch Republican herself ("It is largely our women in the South to-day who keep the black men solid in the Republican party"),[58] Cooper did not, for example, turn her attention to the Farmer's Alliance of the populist movement and its all-to-brief flirtation with interracial radicalism in conjunction with the Colored Alliances.[59] Rather, Cooper's lament was prompted more by her observation that the nation's preoccupation with the plight of, and the threat represented by, laboring, urban immigrant masses had drawn all attention from the oppression of Southern blacks. Their situation was more desperate than Northern workers, their threat to the social order equally ominous—under the proper conditions, Cooper averred, it "would shake this country from Carolina to California."[60] Yet an appeal on their behalf, as offered by Cooper, Harper, Howells, and Cable, eschewed as much as possible the language of radicalism. To introduce equal rights for black Americans into the prevailing social structure of the 1880s and 1890s was to pour new

wine into old skins—and opponents of black civil rights recognized it as such. The friends of racial egalitarianism, however,
while not blind to the implications of their demands (implications
which were often acknowledged in their fictions and in unwary
moments in their nonfictional prose) were checkmated by their
ambivalences. They subscribed to the mores of genteel society—
decency, order, propriety, cleanliness, decorum, and reform—but
were committed to an enterprise which challenged that society
profoundly. Equally certain of the rightness of their cause and the
rightness of their social values, they found themselves wedded to a
radical cause which even they could not call by its proper name.

THREE

The Persistence of Uncle Tom and the Problem of Critical Distinction

I

CENTRAL to understanding the troubles besetting the project of realistic critical definition is an awareness of the persistent influence of Harriet Beecher Stowe's *Uncle Tom's Cabin* during these decades. From its publication in 1852 through the end of the century, the novel remained a bestseller, inspiring admiration from common and elite readers alike. As William Veeder has put it, "what major author was not moved to tribute and tears by *Uncle Tom's Cabin?*"[1] The imaginative scope of Stowe's masterwork led John William De Forest to describe the novel as "the nearest approach to the desired phenomenon [of the great American novel]" yet written and prompted William Dean Howells, well into the realist era, to say that *Uncle Tom's Cabin* was "still perhaps our chief fiction."[2] Other critics, following suit, readily measured the potential social and political effect of novels by comparing them with Stowe's work. As we saw in the previous chapter, the *Century,* when looking for an appropriate benchmark for Howells's achievement in *A Modern Instance,* pointed to *Uncle Tom's Cabin.* While in the opinion of the *Raleigh Observer,* Albion Tourgée's 1879 *A Fool's Errand* was "destined . . . to do as much harm in the world as 'Uncle Tom's Cabin,' to which it is indeed a companion piece."[3]

The host of stage shows engendered by the novel were equally influential. As far as dramatizations were concerned, "the public's craze for *Uncle Tom's Cabin* reached its peak just before the turn of the century."[4] The effect of these shows, however, began almost simultaneously with the novel's publication. Seeing *Uncle Tom's Cabin* on stage was an aesthetic watershed for the young Henry

James, who recalls the experience in *A Small Boy and Others* as an
"aesthetic adventure, . . . a brave beginning for a consciousness
that was to be nothing if not mixed and a curiosity that was to be
nothing if not restless."[5] More troublingly, however, Thomas
Dixon, Jr., author of popular racist romances which included *The
Leopard's Spots* and *The Clansman,* also dated his birth as an author
to the evening he saw a dramatization of Stowe's novel.[6]

For all of these writers the encounter with Stowe seemed both a
shock of recognition and a call for repudiation. In the words of
Anna Julia Cooper, *Uncle Tom's Cabin* had elevated its author to
"the front rank of the writers of her country and age" and had established a standard for American writing. Yet for all its successes
Stowe's fiction had failed to present "an authentic portrait, at once
aesthetic and true to life [of] the black man as a free American citizen."[7] Such responses to Stowe's greatest novel were typical. She
had set a standard that called for its own supersession. Assessments
of her novel became attempts to go Stowe one better, or more specifically, to go *Uncle Tom's Cabin* one better. Efforts in this vein were
central to the shaping of critical dicta and narrative strategies during this period.

Certainly *Uncle Tom's Cabin* was not the only popular cultural influence shaping the literary outlook of writers like James. Veeder
has demonstrated that a wide range of popular materials contributed to James's art and to the art of his "high" culture contemporaries.[8] *Uncle Tom's Cabin,* however, stands out because it was not
merely a best-seller but a work whose political and social effects
were widely acknowledged. For writers like James, Howells, and Cable who believed, albeit in different ways, that fiction could count
heavily in the quest for social betterment, Stowe was an inspiration
and a problem. The success of her novel confirmed the belief that
fiction could achieve social and political ends yet her success
seemed to accommodate a deplorable aesthetic. Her characters
were often sentimentalized, her plot often creaky, and her attention to craft apparently nonexistent. In light of these perceived
failings, the definition of the realistic novel as an instrument for al-
tering social relations could not include an embrace of a sentimental aesthetic. In fact, some of the central tenets of that aesthetic—a
dedication to duty, the valorization of sacrifice and renunciation,
and appeals to the heart rather than the head—were often held up
for critique and ridicule within realistic fiction.

The question of character, however, was central. As realists sought to create characters who were, in Alfred Kazin's words, "wholly merged into their environment,"[9] they found their attempts anticipated to a great degree by *Uncle Tom's Cabin*, which was praised by De Forest for its "truthful outlining of character, [and] natural speaking." De Forest went on to note that "such Northerners, as Mrs. Stowe painted, we have seen; and we have seen such Southerners, no matter what the people south of the Mason and Dixon's line may protest; we have seen such negroes." Yet his admiration of Stowe's delineation of character did not also prevent him from including characterization as one of the novel's most egregious faults. Little Eva was unreal, "a girl such as girls are to be, perhaps, but are not yet." And Uncle Tom was equally idealized: "We have seen such negroes," he observed, "barring of course, the impeccable Uncle Tom."[10]

As this double-edged criticism reveals, Stowe's work was a mixed bag. Its attempt to reveal to its readers the systemic evils of slavery and the effects of such factors as geography on behavior is so compelling that one scholar has attributed to her "an awareness [of the relationship between character and environment] unmatched in American literature until Naturalism fifty years later."[11] Though this may overstate the case, it is true that *Uncle Tom's Cabin* makes clear the connection between behavior and surroundings. Augustine St. Clare's moral lassitude, Miss Ophelia's puritanical hypocrisy, and Sambo and Quimbo's cruelty all arise from the distinct aspects of the respective environments in which these characters are embedded. In like manner, the selling and auctioning of Uncle Tom provide examples of how the larger social system can act to compromise and subvert individual actions and beliefs. Yet while living among individuals who behave in a manner that contradicts their beliefs or who tacitly condone such behavior in others, Tom and Eva remain uncompromised, their spirits and actions untouched by the moral corruption and hypocrisy that surround them, their very purity belying the notion that environment determines character.

A social world in which the primary figures function as exceptions to the laws governing those who surround them is characteristic of the sentimental "issues" novel of the mid-nineteenth century by writers like Stowe and Charles Dickens. (Dickens's work enjoyed extraordinary popularity in the United States, and like *Un-*

cle Tom's Cabin, his novels were often dramatized.) The unsullied heroes and heroines in these works stood outside the social forms that sought to enclose them. On the one hand, slavery, poverty, or prison accounted for the unsocialized status of these characters. Dickens's Little Dorritt, brought up in the Marshalsea, is not a product of larger society. As a young woman she has had "no knowledge even of the common daily tone and habits of the common members of the free community who are not shut up in prisons." But neither is she a product of the Marshalsea. She differs greatly from her brother and her sister and her father in a manner not attributable to social forces. As Dickens explains, "It is enough that she was inspired to be something which was not what the rest were, and to be that something, different and laborious, for the sake of the rest. Inspired? Yes. Shall we speak of the inspiration of a poet or a priest, and not of the heart impelled by the love and self-devotion to the lowliest work in the lowliest way of life!"[12] Dickens's recourse to inspiration is important. The existence of these characters must be something of an enigma; if it were otherwise the novel's social critique would be severely compromised. The virtues of the central character could then be construed as products of the social environment. Among her family members, Little Dorritt is the only one to be born in prison, and it is conceivable that some doctrinaire advocate of debtors' prisons might have claimed that Little Dorritt's admirable qualities provided justification for the practice of incarcerating debtors: not inspiration, but her early experience in prison had instilled in her the virtues of hard work, thrift, and altruism. Dickens's social critique could then be turned on its head.

But whether or not Dickens encountered such criticism, Stowe did. Some contemporary and postwar Southern critics of *Uncle Tom's Cabin* charged that Stowe had simply misinterpreted her own evidence.[13] Uncle Tom's goodness, they argued, was created by the benevolent paternalism of the slave system. "He was all he was, by virtue of his condition as a slave," Francis Shoup proclaimed in the *Sewanee Review* in 1893.[14] Slavery had been a necessary school for benighted Africans, an institution that had begun the laborious project of civilizing the savage.

In Stowe's view, of course, Uncle Tom, like Little Dorritt, was an inspired being. Stowe, in fact, was willing to believe the entire race from which Tom sprang more likely to be inspired than was the

dominant Anglo-Saxon race (although for the sake of the argument against slavery the other black characters in her novel do exhibit the scars of their servitude).[15] Postbellum aesthetics, however, called for changes. In the realistic world of the 1870s, 1880s,
and 1890s, "a world without miracle, without transcendence even
if the individual may have preserved a personal religious faith,"[16]
Uncle Tom, too, became, in the eyes of Northerner and Southerner alike, vulnerable to "his condition as a slave."

The belief that the ex-slave remained a creature of his conditions was central to De Forest's critique of *Uncle Tom's Cabin* in his
novel *Miss Ravenel's Conversion,* which he published the year before
his essay "The Great American Novel" appeared in *The Nation.* In
that novel Dr. Ravenal, one of the central characters, assures a
credulous minister that "Uncle Tom is a pure fiction. There never
was such a slave, and there never will be. A man educated under
the degrading influences of bondage must always have some taint
of grossness and lowness." In place of Tom, De Forest offers his
readers the figure of Major Scott, a "tolerably exemplary black,"
whose sham title, marital infidelities, and bombastic style contrast
markedly with the homespun, humble faithfulness of Stowe's character.[17] In contrast to the death of Uncle Tom, which evokes the
redemptive potentialities of Christian sacrifice and brings into
sharp focus the psychosexual undercurrents in nineteenth-century
thinking about slavery, Major Scott's death seems almost inciden-
tal to De Forest's tale. The Major dies in an exchange of fire with
a Texas Butternut soldier—an exchange that saves no one and that
brings the war no closer to an end.

But the Major's insignificant stature when he is placed beside
Uncle Tom is significant. Indelibly marked by the injustices of his
past servitude, the Major embodies the notion that all doors leading beyond the influences of social institutions are to be closed,
and that if any mode of being exists outside the circle of society,
that mode exerts no civilizing or socializing influence. Redemption is to be sought within and not without the social framework.

As a genre, the sentimental romance assumed that the redemption of the social world lay with the individual: the inspired Little
Dorritt acts "for the sake of the rest," or in Stowe's vision, a United
States senator, in order to behave morally, must forget the laws he
has helped enact and become a man rather than a senator—"man"
in this case being an individual in touch with his feelings. By con-

trast, the realistic novel, albeit with great ambivalence, asserted precisely the opposite: the redemption of the individual lay within the social world. So that even in *Huckleberry Finn,* which devotes so much attention to exposing the shortcomings of society, the action that both completes Huck's mission and prevents him from becoming a social pariah is the socially sanctioned deathbed manumission of Jim.[18]

What Stowe and Dickens accomplished in their novels was an extension of the sway of a single institution—chattel slavery or prison—over all who came into contact with it, only then to exempt central figures from the logical implications of this extension. By contrast, De Forest, Howells, Twain, and James attempted in their works to rescind the exemption—not out of despair but from a faith that to become fully merged with the social world was also somehow to ensure the triumph of the civil and the social.

This realistic faith in the social order, according to Howells, provided "the key-note of the best modern writing in all kinds, and . . . characterized the real literary endeavor of an epoch serious, sympathetic, and conscientious beyond those that have gone before it." In support of his sentiments, Howells quoted approvingly from Josiah Royce's *History of California,* which proclaimed:

> It is the State, the Social Order that is divine. We are all but
> dust, save as the social order gives us life. When we think it
> our instrument, our plaything, and make our private fortunes
> the one object, then this social order rapidly becomes vile to
> us; we call it sordid, degraded, corrupt, unspiritual, and ask
> how we may escape from it forever. But if we turn again and
> serve the social order, and not merely ourselves, we soon find
> that what we are serving is simply our own highest spiritual
> destiny in bodily form. It is never truly sordid or corrupt or
> unspiritual; it is only we that are so when we neglect our
> duty.[19]

Although it is not quite clear whether the social order referred to here is the existing state or some future version of human society, the almost messianic nature of this order is unmistakable. As Howells proclaims on a latter occasion, polite society is "an image of a righteous state on earth."[20] To be outside of society is to be in the realm of the corrupt and the unspiritual.

In Howells's estimation, the qualifications for membership in good society were far from fixed. Society was rapidly expanding to include more and more people who had previously had been excluded. The barriers preventing admittance were tumbling, and no longer did admission require esteemed parentage. In fact, "all that society now asks of people is that they shall behave civilly, and join the rest in doing and saying pleasant things to one another."[21] And as he declared the doors of "good society" open to former outcasts, Howells also acknowledged that many of the seemingly civilized were anything but. Although many members of middle-class nineteenth-century America were only too willing to identify savagery and barbarism with ethnic immigrants and blacks,[22] Howellsian realism made a concerted effort to unfix the barbaric from ethnic identification and set it floating throughout the social body—a notion expressed by Bromfield Corey in *Silas Lapham*:

> It's a curious thing, this thing we call civilisation. . . . We think it is an affair of epochs and of nations. It's really an affair of individuals. One brother will be civilised and the other a barbarian. I've occasionally met young girls who were so brutally, insolently, wilfully indifferent to the arts which make civilisation that they ought to have been clothed in the skins of wild beasts and gone about barefoot with clubs over their shoulders. Yet they were of polite origin, and their parents were at least respectful of the things that these young animals despised."[23]

Instead of an overarching force exerting its power evenly upon the whole of the social body, civilization seems almost capricious, affecting one family member while missing another. Howells even goes on to say elsewhere that civilization also operates only intermittently upon single individuals: "No man can be said to be thoroughly civilized nor always civilized. . . . the most enlightened person has his moods, his moments of barbarism."[24] Although the representation of civilization as a sort of piecemeal process seems to contradict the faith in the social order alluded to earlier, it must be seen in the context of Howells's argument that civilization comes through literature, specifically realistic literature. What one reads shapes one's tastes and determines the degree to which one is civilized.

Although the main engine driving this argument was Howells's effort to create a market for the kind of fiction he was writing, another factor was his attempt to democratize American civilization. As Amy Kaplan has observed, Howellsian realism asserted that there could be a meeting ground for the multifarious members of the American social scene.[25] The partial barbarization of high society and indeed of the self was accompanied inversely by a "genteelization" of the outsider. If one was already consorting with people "who ought to have been clothed in the skins of wild beasts," it was no large step to begin consorting with someone, who though of a different race and class, was at least somewhat well read and respectably clothed.

Turning the critical lens on those white Americans assumed to be members of society while calling into question their claims to membership became a favored tactic of civil rights progressives in their assault on racial barriers. George Washington Cable maintained that "distinctions on the line of color are really made not from any necessity, but simply for their own sake—to preserve the old arbitrary supremacy of the master class over the menial without regard to the decency or indecency of appearance or manners in either the white individual or the colored." Racial discrimination prevented the Southerner from "making and enforcing that intelligent and approximately just assortment of persons in public places and conveyances on the merits of exterior decency that is made in all other enlightened lands."[26]

Arguments like Cable's against discrimination became common to the attack on legal discrimination. Du Bois, for example, produced a similar complaint against the color line, noting that "segregation by color is largely independent of that natural clustering of social grades common to all communities." Naturalizing class distinctions, Du Bois elaborated by saying that the unnatural assortment of individuals based solely on race was contributing to the worsening of racial relations, because "in nearly every Southern town and city, both whites and blacks see commonly the worst of each other".[27] Similarly in Charles Chesnutt's *The Marrow of Tradition,* Dr. William Miller, a fair-skinned, educated black man, after being forced to sit in a Jim Crow car, looks upon his fellow blacks and observes that "personally, and apart from the mere matter of racial sympathy, these people were just as offensive to him as to the whites in the other end of the train. Surely, if a classification of passengers on trains was at all desirable, it might be made upon some

more logical and considerate basis than a mere arbitrary, tactless, and, by the very nature of things, brutal drawing of a color line."[28]
The limitation of this aspect of antisegregation arguments is obvious. These critics accepted too readily a view of class distinctions as a natural division among human beings. In many respects, the efforts to emphasize class distinctions rather than racial ones differed little from tactics of conservative Southerners in the immediate postwar period who sought to maintain their position atop the social order by attempting "to distinguish between classes of the [black] race, to encourage the 'better' element, and to draw it into a white alliance."[29] On the other hand, one should not miss the fact that these desegregation arguments did attempt to define admittance into the social order as an active, voluntary process, rather than as a passive, involuntary one. The project of reunifying the nation following the Civil War had foregrounded the question of what constituted citizenship. What were to be the requirements for individuals and states to be readmitted to the Union? What principles must individuals profess before becoming citizens once again?

As a result of disunion, citizenship emerged in outline not as something already there, but as something that needed to be worked out. From the standpoint of those who saw the war as a vindication of democratic principles and abolitionist idealism, the best solution was a definition of citizenship as an assent to egalitarian principles. Writing in the *Atlantic Monthly* shortly after the Civil War, Charles Sumner had urged that "pardons issue only on satisfactory assurance that the applicant, who has been engaged in murdering our fellow-citizens, shall sustain the Equal Rights, civil and political, of all men, according to the principles of the Declaration of Independence, that he shall pledge himself to the support of the national debt; and, that if he be among the large holders of land, that he shall set apart homesteads for all his freedmen."[30] Citizenship required consent to the principles of equal political and economic rights for all men, especially the former slaves. Of course, the actual conditions for readmission did not approach Sumner's plan, and readmission did not come close to being an endorsement of black equal rights. Nonetheless, the question of what made these diverse regions and societies a nation was not laid to rest, and in fact became a key problem for the American novel. How was one to write "the great American novel?"

For Howells the question was to be answered by first acknowledging that "men are more like than unlike one another: let us
make them know one another better, that they may be humbled
and strengthened with a sense of their fraternity."[31] Realism as an
investigation of social manners sought to interpret behavior and
manners, especially the reading of good fiction, as evidence of a
consent to basic equality. In this respect the implicit and explicit
politics of realistic fiction differed little from Du Bois's recommen-
dation that the American Negro Academy push for "such a social
equilibrium as would, throughout all the complicated relations of
life, give due and just consideration to culture, ability, and moral
worth, whether they be found under white or black skins."[32] Howells's essay "Good Society as the Basis of Equality," while admitting
that the presence of good society implied differences between
classes, also asserted that individuals within the best social classes
always treated each other as equals, regardless of differences in
ability, refinement, or wealth. And in his novels he investigated
again and again the social footing upon which such meetings
could take place in ways that approached democratic ideals.[33]

Repeatedly, however, as with the dinner parties in *Silas Lapham*
and *A Hazard of New Fortunes* and the attempts to establish the social union in *Annie Kilburn*, these efforts to bring together individuals from various walks of life fall short of success. Upper and lower-
class characters are discomfited in their endeavors to get along.
Though the failure is often attributed to the condescending attitudes of the more fortunate, those less fortunate bear their share
of the burden as well. Drunkenness, sentimentality, lack of self-re-
straint, and other "vices" make these characters somehow responsible for their failure to enter society on an equal footing. Their intellectual tastes also made them suspect. If reading the proper
novels was to be a prerequisite for social entry, admitting the
"lower" orders would remain a problem. Howells's faith in realism
notwithstanding, he was forced to admit that "inferior romanticists
are still incomparably the most popular novelists."[34]

Given their condition as products of their environments, how
could lower-class individuals exhibit the behaviors and tastes that
would exhibit their assent to the principle of equality that under-
girded good society? In *Silas Lapham* an answer to this question is
suggested by the relationship between Silas and the architect Seymour, who is in charge of the design and construction of Lapham's

ill-fated Back Bay house. As Silas and Seymour discuss the plans for the house, something of a transformation begins to occur in Silas. His coarse ideas about beauty are gradually refined, and he discovers that he can derive some joy from the artistic realm:

> Aesthetic ideas had never been intelligibly presented to him before, and he found a delight in apprehending them that was very grateful to his imaginative architect. At the beginning, the architect had foreboded a series of mortifying defeats and disastrous victories in his encounters with his client; but he had never had a client who could be more reasonably led from one outlay to another. It appeared that Lapham required but to understand or feel the beautiful effect intended, and he was ready to pay for it. His bull-headed pride was concerned in a thing which the architect made him see, and then he believed that he had seen it himself, perhaps conceived it. In some measure the architect seemed to share his delusion, and freely said that Lapham was very suggestive.[35]

The opening portion of the passage points out the educable nature of Lapham, a quality necessary for the fulfillment of the realist agenda which emphasized the role of criticism in communicating artistic principles. The two men share an almost ideal relationship. Silas's willingness to learn foreshadows his openness to the teachings of the Reverend Sewell, who, towards the book's conclusion, uses the wisdom derived from realistic fiction to help Silas choose the proper path out of his dilemma.

Yet midway through the passage the qualities associated with Silas's new knowledge begin to grow more and more ominous. Silas's receptiveness to artistic ideas becomes the catalyst for his pouring more and more money into the ill-fated structure, and his "bull-headed pride" is the reason for his adhering to the artist's design. Then, in both the concluding portions of the passage and in the paragraphs that follow, a number of suspicious words—*delusion, extravagant, novelties,* and *reckless*—begin to crop up. Finally, the discussion of the expenditures for the house modulates into a discussion between Silas and his wife, Persis, about Lapham's involvement in the stock market which ultimately contributes to his financial collapse.

Although it is tempting to see the outcome of Silas's foray into architectural sensibility as an implicit condemnation of Seymour's ideas, the comments which the latter makes in chapter 14 regarding houses at the dinner party imply the rightness of his taste. There seems rather to be a suspicion inherent in this particular novel that complete transformations in individuals are somehow unrealistic and that to transform a man who sees no impropriety in painting garish advertisements on rock outcrops into a gentleman who can discern the aesthetic advantages to be gained by using a particular type of wood in the construction of his dining room would be to strain the limits of credibility.

Having created Lapham as the representative of a certain "type," Howells's novel finds it difficult to imagine him in any other way, and tends to prefer him as a Boston outsider. After financial ruin has forced Silas and his family to return to the Vermont town of Lapham, the narrator remarks of the failed millionaire, "The Colonel . . . was more the Colonel in those hills than he could ever have been on the Back Bay."[36] It appears that the very coherence of the Colonel's self is threatened by the fulfillment of his desires. This is where Leo Bersani's criticism of realism is most on target. Forced to choose between a character who remains true to himself and a character whose self-refashioning would alter both his character and his relationship to the social order, the novel chooses the former.[37]

If sentimentalism depended on characters who could transcend their environments, then realism would by definition highlight the obstacles to transcendence. While the marriage between Silas's daughter, Penelope, and Tom Corey might represent an alliance across class lines that could underscore the sameness of humanity, the acknowledgement of intransigent social difference would be necessary for the project of generic distinction: "It would be easy to point out traits in Penelope's character which finally reconciled all her husband's family and endeared her to them. These things continually happen in novels; . . . But the differences remained uneffaced, if not uneffaceable, between the Coreys and Tom Corey's wife."[38]

Complete effacement of social differences might happen in the world of sentimental fiction, but not in the world of the real. That the differences Howells notes are "not uneffaceable" reveals the guarded optimism of his social vision, which did see social conditions as contingent and not permanent. But even this guarded optimism was sorely tested as Howells surveyed more minutely the fate of the huddled masses. In the mid-1890s Howells found himself prey to the following gloomy sentiments after a walk through New York's most densely populated slums: "I could not see that in itself or in its conditions it held the promise or the hope of anything better. If it is tolerable, it must endure, if it is intolerable, still it must endure. Here and there one will release himself from it, and doubtless numbers are always doing this, as in the days of slavery there were always fugitives, but for the great mass the captivity remains."[39] Howells's recourse to the images of slavery and fugitives, images which in an earlier "Editor's Study" he declared phantoms of a bygone age and inappropriate to the world of realism, reveals the depth of his despair. The gradual melioration of conditions implied by the realistic formula is belied by the metaphor of slavery, whose dissolution required not simply time but a cataclysm.

The pessimistic outlook on social conditions placed the realistic politics of good society at an impasse, especially with regard to race. Poverty and illiteracy remained facts of life for large numbers of black Americans, and crime among the freedmen was a real if exaggerated part of post-Reconstruction America. While Howells could imagine, through the person of Dr. Olney in *An Imperative Duty,* that most black Americans evinced an almost natural gentility that placed them above the level of recent ethnic immigrants, and that this gentility was augmented by a desire "to be like ladies and gentlemen," even staunch black civil rights advocates were often less optimistic. Frederick Douglass in *The Life and Times of Frederick Douglass* charged that black emigration from the South might fail because "the careless and improvident habits of the South cannot be set aside in a generation."[40] W. E. B. Du Bois in his address to the American Negro Academy stated that "the Negro Academy ought to sound a note of warning that would echo in every black cabin in the land: *Unless we conquer our present vices they will conquer us;* we are diseased, we are developing criminal tendencies, and an alarmingly large percentage of our men and women are sexually impure. . . . The Academy should seek to gather about it the talented, unselfish men, the pure and noble-minded women, to fight an army of devils that disgraces our manhood and our womanhood.[41] Whatever the intent of remarks such as these, they could be construed as endorsing caution regarding equality for black Americans.[42] To the extent that Cable was right in claiming that "neither race, or in other words nobody, wants to see the civil rewards of decency in dress and behavior usurped by the common herd of clowns and ragamuffins,"[43] then the exclusion of impoverished and uneducated black Americans from civil society seemed warranted.

Certainly, a fair enforcement of standards of decency would have excluded many whites, as most civil rights advocates were quick to point out, but for Cable and Du Bois the real emphasis lay in the possibility of inclusion. Those blacks and whites outside the circle of society were not permanently excluded; education, civil rights, and economic opportunity could effect real and swift changes in individuals.

If realistic novels provide any indication, however, it was becoming harder to imagine the reality of such changes. Howells's dilemma with Silas and Penelope Lapham illustrates that for a novel to invest itself too fully in changing individuals was to risk a return to romantic and sentimental notions of fiction. Although social differences between classes were "not uneffaceable," the realistic novel had to stress the persistence of such differences, leaving its readers to meditate upon the "fine and impassable differentiations" that constitute "the price we pay for civilization."[44]

Part of that price was redefining the social world from that which could be changed to that which marked individuals, thus rendering them impervious to change. In *Silas Lapham*, Penelope (who is white) illustrates the barriers between her and the Brahmin Coreys by becoming, figuratively, dark, vernacular, and poor. As she puts the matter to her fiancé, Tom Corey, "I am not at all what they would like—your family; I felt that. I am little, and black, and homely, and they don't understand my way of talking, and now that we've lost everything. . . ."[45] To be sure, Penelope is not imagining herself as black; she is, however, registering her social difference from the Boston elites in terms of physical appearance and voice. Her representation of her "uneffaced, if not "uneffaceable," differences from the Coreys as blackness suggests the easy availability of blackness as a symbol of the unassimilable, even when race itself is not a marker of difference.[46]

As the realistic novel sharpened its critique of social discriminations, it began to depend more heavily on the distinctions it challenged—especially with regard to matters of race. Even when the realistic text proffered the gentility of "free men of color" as a sufficient claim for their social inclusion, it also acknowledged a "blackness most dark" lying beyond the reach of redemption, as demonstrated by George Washington Cable's description of Clemence, the superstitious relic of the past in *The Grandissimes:*

> To Clemence the order of society was nothing. No upheaval could reach to the depth to which she was sunk. It is true, she was one of the population. She had certain affections toward people and places; but they were not of a consuming sort.
>
> As for us, our feelings, our sentiments, affections, etc., are fine and keen, delicate and many; what we call refined. Why? Because we get them as we get our old swords and gems and laces—from our grandsires, mothers, and all. Refined they are—after centuries of refining. But the feelings handed down to Clemence had come through ages of African savagery; through fires that do not refine, but that blunt and blast and blacken and char; starvation, gluttony, drunkenness, thirst, drowning, nakedness, dirt, fetichism, debauchery, slaughter, pestilence and the rest—she was their heiress; they left her the cinders of human feeling.[47]

Cable's first sentence says it all. Slavery has prevented most blacks from entering the order of society. Like Stowe's Topsy, who represents "unredeemed African nature," Clemence proves that slavery was not a true system of socialization. Topsy's behavior springs directly from her African nature. Her presence in Stowe's narrative is something of a supplementary argument to the central critique of the enforced separation of families and the systematic subversion of individual goodwill by the workings of the slave order, both of which point to the system itself as the great corrupter. The lesser argument concerning the natural disposition of the African American is somewhat more slippery. The idea that slavery had halted the civilizing of slaves, leaving them heirs of African heritage, points to a singularly negative view of Africanness.[48] The list of Africanisms in Cable's genealogy of Clemence is a litany of humanity's worst ills, the source of which is not slavery but Africa itself. Slavery is a defective social system because it has failed to socialize the African into progressive society. Thus what was begun as an attack on slavery and caste threatened to metamorphose into an attack on the idea of African-American culture.

One can see this confusion about the proper target of realistic social criticism in the thinking of De Forest as well. His novel *Miss*

Ravenel's Conversion is ostensibly a Civil War novel, but it might be more properly viewed as a reminder to the nation of "'the great elementary duty of man in life—that of working for his own subsistence.'" Approximately midway through the novel, Doctor Ravenel, who utters these words, sets about the task of impressing this lesson on a group of freed blacks in Louisiana, with positive but inconclusive results. Then, by the end of the tale, he sermonizes on a similar note to Captain Colburne, his new son-in-law, asserting that "'in working for our own living we are obeying the teachings of this war, the triumphant spirit of our country and age.'"[49]

This admonition is egalitarian in nature, directed towards blacks as well as whites, Northerners as well as Southerners, collegians as well as illiterates. But the learning of a trade or business, which might bring the genteel young man into association with classes of individuals he might not otherwise encounter, proves an ineffective means of reconciling white and black. As the novel heads towards its conclusion, Doctor Ravenel's efforts to rehabilitate black labor fade into the somber-hued past, and he and his daughter's family express little desire to return to Louisiana and pick up the experiment in free black labor which a Confederate counterattack had forced them to abandon. After having emphasized, time and time again, the monumental effort and human patience required to redeem black labor from its slave heritage, and after having affirmed that "'Our consciences, the conscience of the nation, will not be cleared when we have merely freed the negroes. We must civilize and Christianize them,'" the Doctor decides somewhat inconsequently to redeem only himself by setting up a medical practice in New Boston.[50]

The Doctor's decision not to work on behalf of black labor unveils one of the major ambivalences that run throughout De Forest's novel. (Earlier, Captain Colburne, the novel's hero, allows himself to be dissuaded from taking command of a black regiment.) Free labor is white labor and bound labor is racially or ethnically other. The goal of the novel, indeed the war, is to make labor free and white. Moreover, it seems that this can be best accomplished if those whites in leisure pursuits recognize the need to work. Ravenel declares: "'The young man who is now idle now belongs to bygone and semi-barbarous centuries; he is more of an old fogy than the narrowest minded farm-laborer or ditch-digging emigrant,'" suggesting that somehow idleness rather than labor brings the white man closer to the "semi-barbarous" world of the laboring ethnic.[51]

By entering the world of work, the literary- or scientific-minded white youth was not entering a multiethnic world of fellow workers but fleeing from such associations and the hidden dangers they implied. De Forest's praise of labor did not necessarily include the laborers. Despite the fact that they worked for their living, unskilled laborers were, in De Forest's reckoning, equivalent to idlers and best avoided. When explaining to his daughter the peculiarly American practice of setting up housekeeping in hotels, Doctor Ravenel cites a desire to escape encounters with ethnic and enslaved domestics as the chief motive. Living in hotels, Ravenel says, "is a social necessity of American society. So long as we have entrained servants—black barbarians at the South and mutinous foreigners at the North—many American housekeepers will throw down their keys in despair and rush for refuge to the hotels." The dangers of domestic association with bound labor are only too evident to the Doctor. His daughter, Lily, as he reminds us and her throughout the novel, is subtly Africanized. She speaks "Ashantee English," and "Gold Coast dialects." Her common Southern colloquialisms, "poky" and "right nice," are viewed by her father as Africanized speech. Lily herself concurs, saying that "'I must be allowed to use those Ashantee phrases once in a while. . . . We learn them from our old mammies; that is, you know, our old black nurses.'"[52]

While the Doctor's observations and Lily's admission make evident what proponents of black inferiority were only too willing to suppress—that the transplanted Africans had, despite the dislocations of being stolen into slavery, a culture strong enough to influence that of the supposedly superior white race—these same observations horribly confuse the target of the Doctor's disdain. When condemning the Southerners for starting the war, the good doctor conflates both victim and victimizer, calling the war "'this stupid, barbarous Ashantee rebellion.'" Similarly, when describing Southern intransigence he calls the rebels "'ill-informed as Hottentots'" and explains his dissidence from the Southern slave culture by boasting, "'I have had no plantations, no patrimony of human flesh; very few temptations, in short, to bow down to the divinity of Ashantee,'" suggesting that slavery was somehow a metaphysical property of the Africans themselves.[53]

Of course, from one angle the doctor's phobias about slave labor can be seen as a version of the stock abolitionist argument that the institution of slavery corrupted the slave owners as much as it did the slaves themselves. In this case, however, the vices associated with Southern society arise not so much from a system that gives one person absolute authority over another, but from a situation in which the "non-Christian" elements of African society have not been properly transformed by the virtues of free labor and upright Christianity. "'Justice, honesty, mercy, and nearly the whole list of Christian virtues,'" Doctor Ravenel affirms, "'have hitherto been empty names to [the ex-slaves].'"[54] And it is difficult to determine whether Doctor Ravenel and De Forest are more disturbed by the failure of the ruling class to transmit to their bondsmen Christian values or by the "barbaric" culture of the slaves themselves.

Thus the central intrigue of the novel, Lily Ravenel's ill-fated marriage to Colonel Carter and his subsequent liaison with Mrs. Larue, functions as an object lesson in how the thievery, lying, and lack of respect for the sanctity of the marriage bond endemic to the "slave-grown breed" have infected the whole of Southern society. At times the novel suggests that redeeming this society will require something close to total destruction. The Doctor, for example, affirms that "'their slaveholding Sodom will perish for the lack of five just men, or a single just idea. It must be razed and got out of the way, like any other obstacle to the progress of humanity. It must make room for something more consonant with the railroad, electric-telegraph, printing-press, inductive philosophy, and practical Christianity.'"[55] The new industrial, scientific order that the novel foresees will lack the failings of the slaveholding South, and it is not clear whether those failings include the presence of the ex-slaves themselves. One thing is certain: by the end of the novel the freedmen are nowhere in evidence in the new order. There is, however, an Irish nurse to help Lily take care of Little Ravvie. Without any appreciable fanfare, the novel chooses white over black.

The choice that De Forest makes in *Miss Ravenel's Conversion* was perhaps dictated as much by his association with the Free Soil party prior to the war and by his endorsement of a brand of social Darwinism as much as by his critique of Stowe's sentimental characterizations. Whatever the relative weight of these factors, it is clear that they all worked together to suggest that a rapid and radical transformation of uncouth former outcasts into genteel and devout insiders was merely sentimental fiction. Even a novel like Harper's *Iola Leroy*, which was not as vexed as De Forest's by its relationship with *Uncle Tom's Cabin*, was still insisting in 1892 that a national vulnerability to the "heathenism of Africa" had been one of slavery's legacies: "The young colonies could not take into their early civilization a stream of barbaric blood without being affected by its influence."[56]

By insisting that a belief in a black figure "untainted" by its history of servitude was so much sentimental claptrap, realistic criticism had again inadvertently placed its aesthetics athwart its politics. Moving away from *Uncle Tom's Cabin* aesthetically also seemed to entail moving away from the belief that a "previous condition of servitude" should play no role in determining the freedmen's place in the postbellum social order. Rather than endorse the liberation of African Americans from their slave past, realist critical aesthetics tended to view black figures in a troubling manner. They were embodiments of the undeniable effects of the social order on the individual—of the way that the contingent could become permanent. They were also an index of what had gone wrong in the South and of what had gone wrong with the literary aesthetics of the past.

II

Had realistic criticism merely distanced itself from the strategies of characterization that created an Uncle Tom, the political implications of its critique of sentimentalism might not be worth remarking. A belief that the ex-slaves had been shaped by their history of enslavement may not have allowed for saintly ex-bondsmen, but it was not inconsistent with an argument that the United States still bore the responsibility of putting the freedmen on an equal educational and economic footing with their former oppressors. Accordingly, although De Forest's Dr. Ravenel forgets his "responsibility" to reform Southern labor, he never explicitly discredits the enterprise.

The scope of realism's quarrel with Stowe, however, was broader than a dissatisfaction over matters of African-American characterization. Also at issue was the identification of sentimentalism with the figure of the New England female reformer. To be sure, *Uncle Tom's Cabin* had subjected New England idealism to severe criticism by introducing the character of Aunt Ophelia. Nonetheless, the novel and its author provided a point of critique at which the aesthetics of fiction and the political beliefs represented in that fiction seemed inextricable—and it was at this point that realistic novels and criticism often seemed self-contradictory. Despite attempts to separate politics from aesthetics and attempts merely to prune the excesses of their social commitments, realist texts often appeared to condemn the values and traditions their authors otherwise seemed to endorse.

Specifically, from the 1880s onward, the label of sentimentalism could be applied not only to human feelings and a set of literary strategies, but also to any apparently unrealistic political project. Richard Watson Gilder, for example, defended his effort to reunite North and South by saying, "This is truth, and not sentimentalism."[57] And the *Century* went full steam ahead with its project of sectional reconciliation. In the meantime, the failure of Reconstruction had cast ideas of racial egalitarianism in the light of pure folly. In 1893 Owen Wister criticized the Reconstruction period as an "over-sentimental" attempt to change the racial/social order. He then went on to advocate racial separation on public railways.[58] W. A. Dunning concurred, arguing that "the enfranchisement of the freedmen and their enthronement in political power was as reckless a species of statecraft as that which marked 'the blind hysterics of the Celt' in 1789–95." Such recklessness, said Dunning, was a result of the public's following those whose hearts ruled their heads, the "emotionalists" like "Garrison and Sumner and Phillips and Chase [who believed] that abolition and negro suffrage would remove the drag from our national progress."[59] Then, less than two decades into the twentieth century, Madison Grant, in his racist polemic *The Passing of the Great Race or the Racial Basis of European History* (1916), linked the entirety of egalitarian ideals with "sentimentalism." He lamented that

> There exists today a widespread and fatuous belief in the
> power of environment, as well as of education and opportu-
> nity to alter heredity, which arises from the dogma of the
> brotherhood of man, derived in turn from the loose thinkers
> of the French Revolution and their American mimics. Such
> beliefs have done much damage in the past, and if allowed to
> go uncontradicted, may do much more serious damage in the

future. Thus the view that the negro slave was an unfortunate cousin of the white man, deeply tanned by the tropic sun, and denied the blessings of Christianity and civilization, played no small part with the sentimentalists of the Civil War period, and it has taken us fifty years to learn that speaking English, wearing good clothes, and going to school and to church, does not transform a negro into a white man.[60]

In Grant's view the egalitarian ideals that Howells would have endorsed were indistinguishable from a viewpoint that was at its base sentimental. At the same time, however, many of the racist novels which would have supported Grant's criticisms were unabashedly sentimental in form and content, further confusing the relationship between sentimentality as a literary form and sentimentality as a political critique.

Recently Philip Fisher has argued "that from roughly 1740 to 1860 sentimentality was a crucial tactic of politically radical representation throughout western culture." As a representational strategy, sentimentalism effected an "extension of full and complete humanity to classes of figures from whom it has been socially withheld." Fisher goes on to argue that realism was at best an ineffectual political heir to novels like *Uncle Tom's Cabin*. Rather than participating in a radical revision of its own age, the realistic novel retreated into the status of a "high art form" for which an opposition to the popular and "the elimination of sentimentality [were] central goals."[61]

Curious here is the possibility of reading realism's opposition to popular sentimentality in two somewhat contradictory ways. If one assumes, along with Fisher, that sentimental aesthetics entailed a liberal humanistic politics, then the realists' literary critiques of sentimentalism could have had an ironic political charge. Despite Howells's humanistic wish to "widen the bounds of sympathy,"[62] his hostility to sentimentality would have inadvertently undermined the very values he sought to underwrite. Alternately, however, the postbellum career of sentimentalism permits a different reading of the political meaning of realistic antisentimentalism. As Leslie Fiedler's *The Inadvertent Epic* illustrates, sentimentalism, in the years after the Civil War was as ready a tool in the hands of white Southern conservatives and racists as it had been in the hands of Northern abolitionists. In tracing a tradition that in-

cludes *Uncle Tom's Cabin,* Dixon's *The Clansman,* and Margaret
Mitchell's *Gone with the Wind,* Fiedler proposes that the most radical revision of the post-Reconstruction period was the massive sen-
timentalization of the South, which transformed the former rebellious states into sympathetic victims.[63]

Available without its liberal humanist "content," sentimentalism's literary apparatus could then be harnessed to any cause that
could speak persuasively of its disfranchisement and of having
been unjustly despoiled by a stronger force. Sentimentalism,
which scholars have credited with "the creation of the negro for
the popular mind" in ways that made emancipation possible,[64] can
also be said to have created for that same popular mind the "lost
cause" that contributed to undermining the political and social
gains made by black Americans during the post-Civil War period.

Among the other circumstances compromising the humanistic
politics of realistic aesthetics was the recognition by writers like
Howells and James that women figured largely in the audience for
sentimental and romantic fictions. Like Flaubert's Madame
Bovary, women were those readers most likely to have been misled
into adopting false ideals on the basis of having read unhealthy fiction. While some male readers, particularly Southerners, according to Twain, had been similarly deluded by the fiction they read,
realistic novels invested themselves heavily in questioning the
source and the effects of the ideals that moved women to act both
within and without their fictional worlds. Those women engaged
in philanthropic enterprises were especial targets, and important
here is the convergence of Northern realistic and Southern racist
critiques of the female reformer, who as abolitionist, critic, author,
New England school marm, or feminist suffragist endeavoured,
sometimes hypocritically, to impose upon society a set of "imprac-
tical" moral values.

Enabled by Stowe's Miss Ophelia, a "tall square-formed, and an-
gular" parody of probity whom Stowe described as "the absolute
bond-slave of the "ought,"[65] male writers throughout this era
sketched particularly unflattering portraits of those New England
women driven by principle. Though Miss Ophelia learns and
grows over the course of the narrative, it is the initial picture of her
that stuck with readers, giving rise to a host of similar types. In her
wake are Miss Whitewood from De Forest's *Miss Ravenel's Conversion,* a "hermaphrodite soul [of] lean body and cadaverous coun-

tenance"; James's Olive Chancellor from *The Bostonians*, whose moral morbidity was signified by a smile "which might have been likened to a thin ray of moonlight resting upon the wall of a prison"; Howells's Mrs. Meredith from *An Imperative Duty*, who "would consider herself an exemplary person for having done her duty at any cost of suffering to herself and others"; and Dixon's Susan Walker of Boston, whose dubious morality emerged in her face which, "in spite of evident culture and refinement, [had] the expression of a feminine bull dog."[66] Taken together these figures compose a portrait of New England idealism that exposes its morbidity, selfishness, and sexual repression.

At the same time that novelists were composing their critiques of the tradition of New England reform, sweeping economic and demographic changes began to dictate that New England yield some of its intellectual and moral preeminence. The rise of New York City as a literary center, as illustrated by Howells's move from the *Atlantic Monthly* to *Harper's* in the 1880s, and the concurrent success of New York's *Century* magazine were indications of the change in cultural power. That James's critique of New England in *The Bostonians* (1885) was a critical and popular failure while Dixon's more damning 1902 attack was a best-seller may have had as much to do with the changing literary marketplace as with the nature of these narratives. Mid-1880s Boston was still enough of a cultural force and James's selling power was still too much tied to a New England market to make an unsparing critique of Boston the popular success for which James had hoped. By the 1900s, however, success in New England was no longer a prerequisite for national prominence.

The fictional rendering of these changes in a novel like James's *The Bostonians* is a revealing one. James criticizes his Southern hero, Basil Ransom, yet by suggesting that the moral forces opposing Ransom were as bankrupt and suspect as Ransom's own views, *The Bostonians* underscores the weakening of those political and moral restraints that had kept Southern racism in check in the 1860s and early 1870s. In allowing Ransom to triumph as a result both of his own masculine force and the disarray and tactical miscues of his feminist opposition rather than as a result of superior reasoning and moral judgment, *The Bostonians* proved to be a devastatingly accurate reading of the period. Simultaneously, the novel's inability to locate a viable alternative to New England's spent moral tradition illustrates the inability or unwillingness of Northern intellectuals to achieve the clarity of vision and confidence of voice necessary to combat the wholesale destruction of human rights during this period.

The voice which comes to speak for New England moral idealism in *The Bostonians* is that of Verena Tarrant, the young redheaded woman from the West whose power of speech is almost mesmerizing. Her success is readily identified with Stowe's through Miss Birdseye's exclamation that "I have seen nothing like it since I last listened to Eliza P. Moseley." Ms. Moseley, as Basil Ransom makes clear in referring to her as "the cause of the biggest war of which history preserves the record"[67]—paraphrasing Lincoln's "So this is the little lady who made this big war"[68]—is the novel's representative of Harriet Beecher Stowe. And James appears to cement the relationship by giving his fictional author the name of the runaway slave Eliza, who is involved in one of the most theatrical and touching escapes of Stowe's novel.

Though reminiscent of Stowe in speaking on behalf of feminism and egalitarian principles, the qualities of Verena's voice are only obliquely related to any political content. Self-serving as it is, Ransom's belief that Verena "had been stuffed with this trash by her father, and [that] she was neither more nor less willing to say it than to say anything else" (59), is shared to varying degrees by most of the principles in the novel and is borne out by Verena's eventual abandonment of the feminist cause. Her power can be harnessed to any message whatsoever—a portability so noteworthy that Jennifer Wicke has described Verena as "a pure token of publicity, a figure to be used in an infinity of promotions."[69]

But the number of possible promotions available in *The Bostonians* is not infinite. The novel awards the prize of Verena to Basil Ransom, whom Wicke labels a "romantic and atavistic Southerner . . . representative of a defeated cultural style . . . hopelessly quaint and reactionary."[70] By allowing an "atavistic" Southerner to triumph James's novel charts the inability of the New England tradition to resist and repel those other forces with which it was in competition while also participating in the undermining of that resistance. More specifically, in *The Bostonians* James, like Ransom, lays the blame for New England's failure to resist corruption at the door of "feminization." Ransom's most formidable rival for Verena

is Olive Chancellor, a Boston feminist who fails to hang on to
Verena when the latter is wooed by Ransom.

As one seeks to account for Olive's failure, it is instructive to
keep James's aesthetic concerns in mind. Typically, the social and
political ramifications of "the feminine" have their formal correlatives. *The Bostonians* is a satire, and in one of his more lengthy comments on satire, James addresses its use in starkly gendered terms.
While discussing Edith Wharton's *The Custom of the Country* in his
essay "The New Novel," James writes:

> *The Custom of the Country* is at any rate consistently, almost sci-
> entifically satiric, as indeed the satiric light was doubtless the
> only one in which the elements engaged could at all be
> focussed together. But this happens directly to the profit of
> something that, as we read, becomes more and more one
> with the principle of authority at work; the light that gathers
> is a dry light, of great intensity, and the effect, if not rather
> the very essence, of its dryness is a particular fine asperity.
> The usual 'creative' conditions and associations, as we have
> elsewhere languished among them, are thanks to this ever so
> sensibly altered; the general authoritative relation attested
> becomes clear—we move in an air purged at a stroke of the
> old sentimental and romantic values, the perversions with the
> maximum of waste of perversions, and we shall not here at-
> tempt to state what this makes for in the way of esthetic re-
> freshment and relief; the waste having kept us so dangling on
> the dark esthetic abyss. A shade of asperity may be in such
> fashion a security against waste, and in the dearth of dis-
> played securities we should welcome it on that ground alone.
> It helps at any rate to constitute for the talent manifest in *The
> Custom* a rare identity, so far should we have to go to seek an-
> other instance of the dry, or call it perhaps even the hard, in-
> tellectual touch in the soft, or call it perhaps even the humid,
> temperamental air; in other words of the masculine conclu-
> sion tending so to crown the feminine observation.

The oppositions are clearly and invidiously drawn. The qualities
ranged in the territory of the masculine—dryness, hardness, illu-
mination, and intellect—are obviously regarded as superior to
those under the feminine banner—humidity, softness, darkness,

and sentiment. This is not to say that the latter qualities are unnec-
essary; the essay itself gives due praise to the quality of "saturation,"
the state of being "ideally immersed in his [the author's] own body
of reference." The word itself, however, along with James's use of
the term *immersion* clearly places this quality in the realm of the
moist, the feminine. And as James goes on to make clear, saturation is by itself insufficient. The "other half," James continues, "is
represented by the application."[71] He goes on to decry the lack of
this quality in the fictions of a number of the new novelists.

James also insists that bringing together the elements of the
work into a tight focus is an act of authority—a principle. As if taking a hint from the tenor of the word, he goes on to develop
"authority" along martial and monarchical lines. It "purges at a
stroke" until the masculine "crowns" the feminine, fusing his martial and gendered metaphors. Finally, James's metaphorical language points up a conservational property within the masculine.
The feminine and the saturated tend to waste; the masculine elimi-
nates waste—it conserves, and therefore puts a premium on
boundaries and containment. The metaphorical implications of
the passage suggest that the fluid capacities of the feminine have a
somewhat corrosive, destructive quality, tending to wash away
boundaries. The metaphors also resonate in the political sphere
where social demarcations or boundaries constitute a central
plank of conservatism and the corrosion of those boundaries indicates the leveling powers of democracy.

The metaphorical resonances of James's observations reveal
how much the narrative stance presupposes a subject matter.
Within the compass of a paragraph dealing ostensibly with questions of artistic form, James has re-represented what in his own
novel is the battle for Verena: the battle to give form to the fluidity
of her expression. If Verena's speech is to receive any form at all,
the battle would favor the masculine because, in the terms given
above, feminine form is an impossibility or a monstrosity.

Thus, as *The Bostonians* unfolds, James depicts the principles of
the sentimental, abolitionist heritage as self-destructive. Miss Birdseye, whose "displaced spectacles" reflect the "entire history of
New England reform" (31), wanders across James's stage as a sad
reminder of the glorious past of Bostonian social action. At one
point the narrator utters wih shocking impiety that "it would have
been a nice question whether, in her heart of hearts, for the sake

of this excitement, she did not wish the blacks back in bondage" (27). Surrounded by charlatans and panderers to the public taste, she seems incapable of feeling a genuine commitment to anyone or a personal interest in those around her. In inquiring how she reached this state, we find that her somewhat disturbing inability to be personal and truly committed is not a lack of sympathy but the culmination of a process of excess sympathy:

> She had a sad, soft, pale face, which (and it was the effect of her whole head) looked as if it had been soaked, blurred, and made vague by exposure to some slow dissolvent. The long practice of philanthropy had not given accent to her features; it had rubbed out their transitions, their meanings. The waves of sympathy, of enthusiasm had wrought upon them in the same way in which the waves of time finally modify the surface of old marble busts, gradually washing away their sharpness, their details. (25)

Again, feminism and abolitionism are conveyed in terms of liquid metaphors washing away all solid form and all distinction. The process of erosion and dissolution seems the inevitable result of the success of sympathetic power. Then, almost as if to make sure that the reader connects the feminist spirit with a lack of all critical ability, James comments that Miss Birdseye "had not the faintest sense of the scenic or plastic side of life" (28).

To recall Stowe's *Uncle Tom's Cabin,* abolitionist spirit depends on an insistence that the personal sphere should come first despite the calls to sacrifice the personal to the public. Senator Bird in Stowe's novel discovers his duty in regard to the Fugitive Slave Law by placing his personal feelings above his public duties as a senator. In James's exaggerated formulation, however, the insistence upon responding to the suffering of others in a personal way—as if they were members of one's own family—often entails the sacrifice of the needs and feelings of the immediate family in favor of those of the larger human family. The boundaries of the home are pushed so far outward that they have no meaning. Like the senator's wife, Mrs. Bird, who judges everything as a homemaker, Miss Birdseye's "charity began at home" (26). But unlike Mrs. Bird, "whose husband and children were her entire world," Miss Birdseye's concerns "ended nowhere" (26). James's portrait of his relic of abolitionist heritage offers a scenario in which Mrs. Bird,

Stowe's avatar of personal sympathy who gives away her dead son's
clothes to Eliza, might quite easily become Miss Birdseye, who "had
given herself away so lavishly all her life that it was rather odd there
was anything left of her for the supreme surrender" (376).

Though at first glance Miss Birdseye's plight does not seem characteristic of that of the other women in *The Bostonians* the adjec-
tives used to describe her resurface, almost improbably, in connection with other female figures.[72] Doctor Prance, who evokes
"masculine" terms from the narrator—"spare, dry, hard" (39)—
and seems quite different from Miss Birdseye, is nonetheless like
the old crusader in that she too has "no features to speak of" (39).
Similarly, Olive Chancellor, who possesses an ability to discriminate and "sharp and irregular" features is somewhat formless below the face—"she had absolutely no figure" (8). And like their
mentor, these two younger women are intensely unmarried except
to a profession or a cause. Even the grand Mrs. Farrinder shares
with Miss Birdseye an inability to make proper social distinctions,
and Olive accords to her the same provinciality that she attributes
to Miss Birdseye.

James reinforces the links between Miss Birdseye on the one
hand and Olive and Doctor Prance on the other in two ways. First,
he orders his plot so that Doctor Prance and Miss Birdseye perform parallel functions in Ransom's quest for Verena. They both
withhold from Olive information about Ransom's presence and
his intentions. They both listen to the Southerner. On Ransom's
second visit to Boston he encounters Miss Birdseye on the street,
and while accompanying her in a streetcar extracts from her the
whereabouts of Verena and her promise not to tell Olive of their
meeting. Under the delusion that Ransom may become a convert,
she tells him upon boarding a second streetcar, "I won't say anything" (211). Her silence is the first in a chain leading to Verena's
silence about her own walk to Harvard's Memorial Hall with Ransom, and to Doctor Prance's silence when Ransom comes to Mar-
mion in search of Verena.

During his conversation with Doctor Prance, Ransom is explicitly reminded of the first incident with Miss Birdseye and makes a
comparison between the two: "it would be no easier for Doctor
Prance to subscribe to a deception than it had been for her vener-
able patient" (337). Miss Birdseye is, however, deceived, and Doctor Prance, through solicitude for her patient, allows the decep-

tion to continue. The final link in this chain of silences is Verena's aborted speech at the Music Hall—the location of which is first divulged to Ransom by Doctor Prance.

James also connects Miss Birdseye to Olive Chancellor in his descriptions of their homes. Olive's parlor, filled with "so many objects that spoke of habits and tastes" (16), is shaped "exactly" like Miss Birdseye's enormous streetcar—the place where the first betrayal of Olive occurs. The social forms that Olive erects are shown in this linkage to be quite vulnerable to those things she abhors most—her own parlor is where she first extends to Ransom an invitation to visit Miss Birdseye's parlor where the Southerner meets Verena. In fact, the betrayals perpetrated by the other women have at their source the self-betrayal Olive commits by bringing Ransom in contact with the Boston radicals.

All told, the women hold their tongues, while listening to what Ransom has to say, but Ransom, when confronted with Verena's eloquence, listens without listening. For example, he observes that Verena's address in Miss Birdseye's parlor

> was full of schoolgirl phrases, of patches of remembered eloquence, of childish lapses of logic, of flights of fancy which might indeed have had success at Topeka; but Ransom thought that if it had been much worse it would have been quite as good, for the argument, the doctrine, had absolutely nothing to do with it. It was simply an intensely personal exhibition, and the person making it happened to be fascinating. (58)

In his ability to put aside the doctrine of Verena's address, Ransom demonstrates an agile critical faculty. The Southerner is able to make fine discriminations while at the same time extracting an enjoyment from the spectacle. In fact, the descriptions of Ransom are strikingly similar to James's description of himself in attendance at a performance of *Uncle Tom's Cabin*. James recalls that he noticed quite clearly the "audible creak of carpentry" but was also able to mark "where the absurd . . . ended and the fun, the real fun, which was the gravity, the tragedy, the drollery, the beauty, the thing itself, briefly, might be legitimately and tastefully held to begin."[73] It is perhaps here that James's affinity for the character of Ransom is most evident. One might argue that this critical ability is what gives Ransom the final victory in the battle for Verena.

But the book's ending signals that the victory is less than glorious. Despite Ransom's powers of discrimination, he makes a failure of distinction similar to that made by Olive Chancellor when she attributes all that is base about Verena to her parents. He views Verena's sentiments as opinions "she was neither more nor less willing to say . . . than to say anything else" (59). The narrator immediately condemns this aspect of Ransom's thinking, remarking that "I know not whether Ransom was aware of the bearings of this interpretation, which attributed to Miss Tarrant a singular hollowness of character" (58). In making this criticism the text drives home the comparison between Ransom and Olive. If Olive blames Verena's vulgarities on her parents, Ransom "contented himself with believing [Verena] was as innocent as she was lovely" (59). Ransom is also fired by a desire to save Verena from the "raving rabble" (422).

The extent to which Ransom reflects Olive accounts in part for the Southerner's tarnished victory. He is forced to abandon the chivalric ideals he espouses. By the final scene, as Verena gives up her pretence of "loyalty to her cause," Ransom, too, ignores the chivalric/romantic aspects of his position and seeks only to further his own ends. Verena asks him "to go away just as any plighted maiden might have asked any favor of her lover" (422), but Ransom, unlike the chivalric hero, is not inclined to honor the pleas of a maiden.

Nonetheless, Ransom does win the girl, thrusting a hood over her head as he does so. The conclusion may be attributed in part to James's propensity to see the form/content issue in gender related terms, "the masculine tending so to crown the feminine observation." The ending may have also been suggested by James's association of Verena with the undeniable but seemingly wayward power of Stowe's *Uncle Tom's Cabin*. Stowe, of course, disclaimed responsibility for her novel, attributing the composition of the book to the supernatural agency of God. Similarly, Verena denies her role as the originator of her speech, saying, "It isn't *me* mother" (52). The disclaimers are an invocation of higher authority, placing the credit for authorship outside the particular individual.

The danger of such disclaimers was that they allowed verbal expression to be appropriated by whoever might stake a claim. Verena eloquently parrots the opinions of those closest to her. She strikes up alliances with those who are most willing to exert their power over her, and her ability suffers little in the translation. So portable is her power that in the end she and her rehearsed speech are carried off by a man whose opinions are diametrically opposed to Olive's. Like *Uncle Tom's Cabin,* which James viewed as being carried further, carried even violently furtherest" by its dramatizations, Verena, too, was an expression without any particular allegiance to cause or author.[74]

The theatrical performances of *Uncle Tom's Cabin* were staged without Stowe's permission. As Charles Dudley Warner points out, "Mrs. Stowe had neglected to secure the dramatic rights, and she derived no benefit from the great popularity of a drama which still holds the stage."[75] These Uncle Tom shows, which fed upon the melodrama of Stowe's work, were comfortably oblivious to the animus of the original. But even the novel itself was so at home during the period of reaction that Francis Shoup wrote in the *Sewanee Review* some seven years after the publication *The Bostonians* that *Uncle Tom's Cabin* was "a great book—great as a work of art, losing nothing by the total disappearance of the factitious environment which was the sole motive of its production."[76] Before Shoup, Joel Chandler Harris, writing in 1880, blithely referred to Stowe's opus as a "defence of slavery."[77] The unreconstructed Southerner, in fiction and in fact, found it possible to appropriate the ostensibly abolitionist voice for his own ends.

Moreover James, though insisting in "The Art of Fiction" that the "deepest quality of a work lies in the quality of the mind of the producer,"[78] employs in *The Bostonians* a narrator who at key points denies responsibility for the views being expressed. When relating to the reader Ransom's philosophy on women and reform, the narrator feels compelled to remind the reader that "I am but the reporter of his angry *formulae*" (48), reducing himself to a journalist. This realist text is Ransom's mouthpiece. No doubt, James has his own sentiments about his hero, the nature of which scholars and readers of *The Bostonians* have expended considerable labor attempting to discover, with many concluding that James is Ransom.[79] In truth, various aspects of the novel argue against such a conclusion, but the fact that such observations have been made is important in itself. His narrator's disclaimers notwithstanding, James, like his heroine in *The Bostonians,* finds his voice in these interpretations carried away or stifled by an unreconstructed Southerner.

At the turn of the century, critiques of New England's moral heritage proved extremely useful to Southern voices. The purported warping effects of the reform tradition on femininity was picked up by Thomas Dixon, Jr., in *The Leopard's Spots* in the person of "Susan Walker of Boston, whose liberality had built the new Negro school house and whose life and fortune was devoted to the education and elevation of the Negro race."[80] She is another example of the New England reformer, and as is the case in James's novel, the reader is encouraged to question or discount the femininity of such women. "'Lay aside your Don Quixote Southern Chivalry this morning,'" Susan Walker tells the Reverend John Durham, "'and talk to me in plain English. It doesn't matter whether I am a woman or a man'" And the Reverend, perhaps a little more eager than James's Ransom in his dealings with Olive, responds with some relish: "'You ask me for plain English. I will give it to you'" (46). He then tells her that her mission to educate the black freedmen is misguided, self-righteous, and so dangerous that he would like to "'box you up in a glass cage, such as are used for rattlesnakes, and ship you back to Boston'" (47). The modulation from treating a woman like a man to treating a woman like an animal is meant to underscore the perceived threat that these New England women posed to the social order. Like Howells's Miss Meredith in *An Imperative Duty,* such women were ruthlessly virtuous and "would be capable of an atrocious cruelty in speaking or acting the truth,"[81] which is to say, their version of the truth.

Not one for understatement, Dixon goes on to make sure that the reader connects the "unnatural" leadership of the South during Reconstruction with the "damned feminization" of the postwar period by presenting the reader with the unlikely picture of a Simon Legree who has survived the war by dressing as a woman. "He shaved clean, and dressed as a German emigrant woman. He wore dresses for two years, did house work, milked the cows, and cut wood for a good natured old German. He paid for his board, and passed for a sister just from the old country" (85). The conjunction of false femininity, working-class immigrant status, and a New England pedigree in the person of the resurrected Legree, who then goes on to become Speaker of the House in the North Carolina legislature, also predetermines the terms in which the redemption of the South will be couched: masculine, professional, and Southern.

Thus at the key election when the conservative ticket soundly defeats the "carpet-bagger" ticket led by Legree, the Klan takes matters into its own hand, ordering its members to

> visit every negro in the county, and warn every one as he values his life not to approach the polls at this election. Those who come, will be allowed to vote without molestation. All cowards will stay at home. Any man, black or white, who can be scared out of his ballot is not fit to have one. Back of every ballot is the red blood of the man that votes. The ballot is force. This is simply a test of manhood. It will be enough to show who is fit to rule the state. (160)

"Simply a test of manhood" are the words used by Major Decameron, who is seconded in his efforts by preachers, doctors, and other community leaders. Never mind that the white populace is not put under similar threat of violence, the test is one of manhood, and the freedmen who have reigned in an era marked by the prominence of "unnatural" Northern femininity stand no chance. The racial issue is subsumed by the question of gender, which in turn is used to "naturalize" the new social order.

Here one might point to how widespread was this notion of the ordering power of the masculine in late-nineteenth century fiction, generic differences notwithstanding. From De Forest's Captain Colburne to Howells's Silas Lapham to James's Basil Ransom to Dixon's Charlie Gaston, the heroes of the nineteenth-century novel continually rediscover the virtues of their natural "manhood." Even in a text so marked by subtleties as James's *The Ambassadors*, Lambert Strether's surpassing of Maria Gostrey as an intelligent observer provides yet another instance of the "masculine conclusion tending to crown the feminine observation." More importantly, Strether's growth is a process of breaking the ties that link him to Mrs. Newsome.

In response to this assault on the New England tradition of feminist reform, many liberal and progressive voices on race felt a need to include in their various agendas defenses and praise of the New England tradition and the feminist reformers who embraced it. Tourgée's *A Fool's Errand* and *Bricks without Straw* spoke favorably on behalf of the "pure-hearted Northern girls [who] taught . . . the race which had just now its first chance at the tree of knowledge."[82] In one of her essays, Pauline Hopkins, African-American novelist and activist, proclaimed melodramatically,

"May my tongue cleave to the roof of my mouth and my right hand forget its cunning when I forget the benefits bestowed upon my persecuted race by noble-hearted New England."[83] And W. E. B. Du Bois, in *The Souls of Black Folk,* called the New England effort to educate the freedmen "the finest thing in American history." In his view, "the crusade of the New England school ma'am" was a tale waiting to be told:

> The annals of this Ninth Crusade are yet to be written,—the tale of a mission that seemed to our age far more quixotic than the quest of St. Louis seemed to his. Behind the mists of ruin and rapine waved the calico dresses of women who dared, and after the hoarse mouthings of the field guns rang the rhythm of the alphabet. Rich and poor they were, serious and curious. Bereaved now of a father, now of a brother, now of more than these, they came seeking a life work in planting New England schoolhouses among the white and black of the South. They did their work well. In that first year they taught one hundred thousand souls, and more.[84]

The nation, however, was more ready to be moved by the story of a South unfairly beset by corrupt Reconstruction governments and the venal depredations of black men than by the trials of reform-minded women. A sweeping reassessment of that period would have to wait until 1935 when Du Bois published his *Black Reconstruction.* In regard to the spirit of abolition and equality, the fin de siècle was a period of critique.

As noted earlier, both James and Dixon made their experience of viewing dramatizations of *Uncle Tom's Cabin* central to their aesthetic development. In his autobiographical *A Small Boy and Others,* James locates the "brave beginning for a consciousness that was to be nothing if not mixed and a curiosity that was to be nothing if not restless," on the evening of his attending a production of *Uncle Tom's Cabin* at the National Theatre.[85] He recalled with particular vividness the staging of Eliza's dramatic escape across the ice floes of the Ohio River. Correspondingly, when James came to assess his success in writing *The Ambassadors,* Stowe's *Uncle Tom's Cabin* came to be a standard of measure. In the preface to the novel he claimed that "no dreadful old pursuit of the hidden slave with bloodhounds and the rag of association can ever, for 'excitement,' I judge, have bettered it at its best."[86] By assuming the role of slave catcher in his pursuit of his subject, James seemingly signals his triumph over Stowe's compositional methods.

Likewise Dixon figured the scene of Eliza's escape as a scene of capture rather than one of freedom. In Dixon's novel, George Harris, Jr., a recreation of Eliza's Little Harry, finds himself on "the spot where his mother had climbed up the banks of the Ohio River into the promised land of liberty, and followed the track of the old Underground Railroad for fugitive slaves a few miles. He came to a village which was once a station of this system. Here strangest of all, he found one of these ash-heaps in the public square" (403). The "ash-heap" is the residue of a lynching where a black man has been burned to death. In the strange odyssey of George Harris, Jr., the freedom won during the Civil War has proved a cruel illusion. Hugh Halliday, a scion of the Quaker Household that helped Eliza and Harry escape the slave catchers, finds himself, too, within the power of Legree.

The reversal of Stowe's central image of pursuit, of despoiler and despoiled, is perhaps Dixon's single most powerful tropological inversion of Stowe. The rape or threatened rape of slave women is transformed into that of white women by lustful free black men. The attempt by the black majority leader, Tim Shelby, to force Mollie Graham to kiss him is the event that conjures, "like magic in a night," the Ku Klux Klan, which saves civilization. Similarly, Dick's rape of Flora is the event that catalyzes the radical defeat of populism in book 3. And if James as a critic of his *The Ambassadors* could say that no pursuit of slave by bloodhounds could have bettered "for excitement" his quest for his story, so many a critic agreed that Dixon's transformation of the trope of pursuit had gone quite beyond Stowe.

Despite their obvious differences, Southern romancer and Northern realist could cite similar concerns and interests. Like James, Dixon compared his work as a novelist to the office of historian, proclaiming that in *The Leopard's Spots* "the only serious liberty I have taken with history is to tone down the facts to make them credible in fiction."[87] Additionally, according to Dixon's biographer, the novel was originally called "The Rise of Simon Legree," a title suggested by Howells's *The Rise of Silas Lapham*.[88] Dixon was also not the only Southerner to evoke Howells. Even Thomas Nelson Page could declare Howells a kindred spirit,[89] further illustrating that the rhetoric of realism could be deemed applicable to a host of works whose spirit was not in accord with that of Howells or James.

James attributed such problems of critical distinction to an over-abundance of literary criticism. In his opinion the proliferation of periodical magazines had so stimulated the production of uninformed criticism that the first act of discrimination—simply refusing to notice a work's existence—was never made. The British and American world had failed to learn from the French literary scene where "they publish hundreds of books which are never noticed at all" because "it is recognized that such volumes have nothing to say to the critical sense, that they do not belong to literature, and that the possession of the critical sense is exactly that which makes it impossible to read them and dreary to discuss them—places them, as a part of critical experience, out of the question." But the demands of the periodical marketplace on the Anglo-American critical scene made it impossible to rule a body of texts "out of the question." Periodical literature, James complains, "is like a regular train which starts at an advertised hour, but which is free to start only if every seat be occupied. The seats are many, the train is ponderously long, and hence the manufacture of dummies for the seasons when there are not passengers enough. A stuffed mannikin is thrust into the empty seat, where it makes a creditable figure till the end of the journey." The train as a figure for public vulgarity and production for the market is obvious enough. The trope of the mannikin, however, is somewhat misleading as regards James's ultimate point. Though a passenger might be disconcerted upon discovering at the end of his journey that some of his fellows are not real people, one would also expect that the psychic effects of this discovery on such a passenger would be temporary—a momentary discomfort. But as we read James's remonstrance we find that the threat is indeed quite sinister and potentially long-lasting. The proliferation of criticism "may be as fatal as an infectious disease" because "literature . . . like other sensitive organisms, . . . is highly susceptible of demoralization . . . and the consequence of its keeping bad company is that it loses all heart."[90]

The "case," to use James's word, is not simply that of a brief, perhaps unpleasant surprise at finding out a fellow passenger is a nonperson—of having been in the presence of no company at all. Rather, the passenger/reader discovers that he has been in the presence of bad company that both disheartens and demoralizes.

The false body of the mannikin, sitting rather innocuously in its seat, is reinterpreted by James as a diseased body that threatens to spread contagion to the real passengers.

As we have seen in reference to the various arguments surrounding Jim Crow legislation, the fear of suffering harmful effects from forced association with unworthy others plays a central role in the writings about race. In both social and literary criticism these fears found a common ground in American railroad trains and stations. According to Cable, American conveyances were more uncomfortable than their European counterparts because they were segregated by race rather than by class. In his turn, James launched what was for him a serious indictment of Anglo-American criticism by lamenting, "We blunder in and out of the affair as if it were a railway station—the easiest and most public of the arts."[91]

To push the analogy a little further, what such fears made necessary was the presence of a discerning conductor empowered to decide who should gain entrance into the railway car and who should be excluded—what was needed was person able to decide which people were real and which were mannikins. It is precisely such a conductor that we find in James's critical prefaces where many a "naive" reader has discovered to his dismay that some of James's personages are not indeed real creatures—that "Maria Gostrey and Miss Stackpole . . . may run beside the coach 'for all they are worth,' they may cling to it till they are out of breath (as poor Miss Stackpole all so visibly does), but neither all the while, so much as gets her foot on the dusty step, neither ceases for a moment to tread the dusty road."[92]

The conductor has done his work assiduously. Of course James has made his job easier by transforming the railroad car to a personal coach, but such a switch of vehicles was indicative of the way that ostensibly private prejudices during this period were coming to define public space. When responding to the charge that the separate car law violated the Thirteenth Amendment to the Constitution, Justice Joseph Bradley made a similar switch, arguing that "it would be running the slavery argument into the ground to make it apply to every act of discrimination which a person may see fit to make as to the guests he will entertain, or as to the people he will take into his coach or cab or car."[93]

What James and Howells wanted their fellow citizens to see was that the quality of their society depended on the willingness of

Americans to become discriminating critics. For James there was
the desire to persuade his audience that popular tastes could be re-
configured and reshaped for different aesthetic ends; for Howells
there was the hope that Americans would bring to bear the truths
of realistic literary practice against the antiegalitarian fictions of
the past. But if it were possible to rework conventions, then
couldn't the supposedly outmoded conventions of the past be re-
worked for the present? Could not "the knightly warrior type,
. . . not the flashy traveling salesman, not the jaded aesthete, not
the agonized, overcivilized intellectual . . . [be] the stuff of which
the nation was made"?[94] If James measured himself against the
thrill of romantic and sentimental conventions, then why could
not the nation as a whole—although not for the purpose of critique but for emulation?

Egalitarianism, too, seemed to fly in the face of the need to discriminate. W. A. Dunning argued that "slavery had been a *modus
vivendi* through which social life was possible; and that, after its disappearance, its place must be taken by some set of conditions
which, if more humane and beneficent in accidents, must in essence express the same fact of racial inequality."[95] Racial segregation of American public space provided this new set of conditions.
Like the slavery apologists before them, segregationists had at
hand a variety of sources—religious, scientific, and historical—to
draw upon for arguments, strategies, and rationales for dividing
the nation along racial lines. What also aided segregationists in the
post-Reconstruction era, however, was that progressive voices, including the realistic novel, not only helped discredit the abolitionist legacy, but also conceded the central conservative argument
that social discrimination was unavoidable. All that remained was
to determine the criteria for making discriminations. Without
powerful Northern voices willing to challenge American racism,
the fine distinctions of deportment, demeanor, and taste put forward by realists and civil rights activists stood little chance of prevailing. For the majority of white Americans, black and white racial
difference appeared to be the most sensible way to bring order to
an unruly social scene.

FOUR

Black and White Strangers

I

WHILE in the eyes of many white observers, the nation's endorsement of Jim Crow laws, especially in regard to public and private conveyances in the South, should have solved its major social problem, Henry James's *The American Scene* suggested otherwise. Chronicling the writer's impressions of his native land upon his return in 1904, the book severely censures American society. Encapsulating James's indictment of the United States was an embittered and extended apostrophe to the Pullman in which he had made his journey to the Southern states. The railroad exemplified for James the failure of American society to fulfill its promise of civilization. Haste, vulgarity, and ugliness were the legacy of a society that had impressed James more with what it had left undone than with what it had done. Focusing his ire not on the locomotive but on the Pullman, which was a place of habitation as well as transportation, James made these cars representative of the civilization of which America was boasting. The Pullman was "the great symbolic agent" in which were carried, "if not Caesar and his fortune, at least almost *all* facets of American life."[1] On the whole, the people that it did carry were too much like one another for James's taste—too steeped in trade to be little more than exemplars of the triumph of vulgarity and lowness and the absence of social distinction.

Had he been so inclined, James's search for "that part of the national energy that is not calculable in terms of mere arithmetic" (*A*, 389), might have led him to a prolonged encounter with the literature of black America. Despite the fact that the Gilded Age's gospel of progress and prosperity had found endorsements from Frederick Douglass, until his death in 1895, and from Booker T.

Washington, whose address to the Atlanta Cotton Exposition later that same year sought to secure black economic participation in the new industrial South, some black American intellectuals had been voicing criticisms of the Gilded Age, at least as early as 1892 with the publication of Frances Harper's *Iola Leroy*. The closing decades of the nineteenth century may have been known for producing an unprecedented number of millionaires, but Harper's heroine had a ready answer to the query whether "the world [was] most indebted . . . to its millionaires or to its martyrs. . . . "'To be,' continued Iola, "the leader of a race to higher planes of thought and action, to teach men clearer views of life and duty, and to inspire their souls with loftier aims, is a far greater privilege than it is to open the gates of material prosperity and fill every home with sensuous enjoyment.'"[2] The American home, as Iola shrewdly observed, had become a place of conspicuous consumption. He or she who could help fulfill these newly created desires could profit handsomely. Untold riches were at hand, but racial service and leadership mandated that black elites forego the new paths to economic success. The higher calling was the way of renunciation and sacrifice. Harper's novel, however, was making a virtue of necessity. In the words of Professor Langhorne, a scholar from Georgia who speaks at a council on the welfare of black Americans: "How many of us to-day . . . would be teaching in the South, if every field of labor in the North was as accessible to us as to the whites?" (*I*, 248). The path of racial service was the only one available; few of those favored by the creation of new avenues to prosperity happened to be black.

In recompense, however, there were the virtues of black solidarity and black identity. Again, to quote Professor Langhorne, "this prejudice, by impacting us together, gives us common cause and brings our intellect in contact with the less favored of our race" (*I*, 248). Additionally this recompense was not merely compensation but reward beyond measure. It was the key to avoiding self-estrangement. "Masquerading as a white man" was a sure path to becoming a "moral cripple." (*I*, 203, 266). While white identity promised "a life of careless ease and pleasure," life as a black American would have "a much grander significance" (*I*, 274).

The economic liabilities of black racial identity could be inflected differently, as illustrated by Albion Tourgeée. In his brief on behalf of Homer Plessy, Tourgée had asked whether, in a society premised upon the denial of basic civil and economic rights to African Americans, it is "possible to conclude that the reputation of being white is not property? Indeed, is it not the most valuable sort of property, being the master-key that unlocks the golden door of opportunity?"[3] Harper's novel concurred on this point, asserting that "to be born white in this country is to be born to an inheritance of privileges, to hold in your hands the keys that open before you the doors of every occupation, advantage, opportunity, and achievement" (I, 265–66). In the race to riches, being black was a decided handicap. But where Tourgée's brief sought to secure for Plessy the rights of property that racial distinctions were denying him, Harper treated such opportunities as incipient Faustian bargains.[4] Correspondingly in *Iola Leroy* the plot repeatedly calls upon its light-skinned African-American characters to choose between material prosperity—embodied in a white identity—and moral duty—embodied in a black one. Iola, her uncle Robert, her brother Harry, and her eventual husband, Dr. Latimer, each refuse opportunities to suppress the fact of their partial black ancestry in favor of material benefits. We are told, for example, that Dr. Latimer's wealthy paternal grandmother had "made overtures to receive him as her grandson and heir" if he would "forsake his mother's people" (I, 238). Moved by Latimer's striking "resemblance to her dear departed son," the grieving woman declares herself willing to overlook her grandson's mixed racial heritage if he will agree to overlook it as well. The reader is assured, however, that the young physician had "nobly" declined the offer. In the story he ultimately comes to displace the white Dr. Gresham as Iola's suitor. The two eventually marry and then embark jointly on a life of service to the race—in effect turning their backs upon the values of the Gilded Age.

As far as James was concerned, however, there was no reason that he should have been aware of Harper's novel, which was published twelve years before he returned to the United States, and which was not reviewed in major white journals. Harper's voice could have easily been lost in the disconcerting din that confronted James on his homecoming. And had he heard it, its sentimental overtones, its use of dialect, and its didactic moralism would not, despite its dissent from the doctrine of material wealth, have identified it as a potential ally for the "restless analyst" of *The American Scene* (A, 25).

William James, however, had made sure that his brother would not miss entirely the notes sounded by black America. As Henry prepared for his Atlantic crossing, William mailed him a copy of the newly published *The Souls of Black Folk*, telling him, "I am sending you a decidedly moving book by a mulatto ex-student of mine, Du Bois, professor of history at Atlanta (Georgia) negro College. Read Chapter VII to XI for local color, etc."[5] It is easy to imagine how Henry James's reading of *The Souls of Black Folk* could have been one of the signal moments in American literary history, bringing together the novelist who was redefining the contours of American fiction and the scholar/novelist/activist who was articulating a new vision of African Americanness. As part of James's reintroduction to his native land, *The Souls of Black Folk* might have suggested an alternate trajectory for *The American Scene* such that its criticism of a society scored by commercialism might have also become a powerful brief against American racism. William, as we have seen, had inveighed publicly against lynching on two separate occasions, impressing on his readers the urgency of putting a halt to the violence against African Americans. Henry, as he traveled South, saw evidence to confirm the pervasiveness of the lynching spirit. Accompanied through Richmond by an unreconstructed young Southerner, Henry is made to understand that though his companion "wouldn't have hurt a Northern fly, there were things (ah, we had touched on some of these!) that, all fair, engaging, smiling, as he stood there, he would have done to a Southern negro" (*A*, 389). The benign aspect that Southern whites turned to their Northern counterparts did not bother to conceal the virulence of their enmity toward blacks. Despite this conversation, James elsewhere in *The American Scene* discounts the influence that his voice or any other might have in ameliorating the racial situation in the South. Whatever the available wisdom about improving race relations, "the lips of the non-resident were, at all events, not the lips to utter this wisdom". "Silence," James avers, is a preferable policy (*A*, 376).

One need only turn to "The After-Thought" of *The Souls of Black Folk* to see how disappointing this silence would necessarily have been to Du Bois. Leaving his reader with the plea to "*vouchsafe that this my book fall not still-born into the world-wilderness,*" Du Bois had invested the success of his project in the willingness of his readers to respond with "thought" and "thoughtful deed."[6] *The American Scene* is nothing if not thoughtful, but its handling of the race problem falls dreadfully short of the clear denunciations of lynching and mob violence that prevailing conditions called for. In addition, the voice of *The Souls of Black Folk* would have been somewhat critical of James's methods. Du Bois had warned his reader that the truth about the black South would likely elude the casual observer. He cautioned that "to the car-window sociologist, to the man who seeks to understand and know the South by devoting the few leisure hours of a holiday trip to unravel the snarl of centuries,—to such men very often the whole trouble with the black fieldhand may be summed up by Aunt Ophelia's word 'shiftless'" (*S*, 469). Du Bois's invocation of Stowe's Aunt Ophelia from *Uncle Tom's Cabin* points up the problem of the North's critical stance toward African Americans. A woman of principle and duty, Miss Ophelia cannot at first bear to touch Topsy, and until she learns from the example of Little Eva, she is unable to have any effect on Topsy's behavior. If one gets closer one will see a truer picture. The apparent shiftlessness of black laborers (Du Bois describes two young men who present "a happy-go-lucky, careless picture of irresponsibility"), is simply apparent: "they are not lazy; to-morrow they'll be up with the sun; they work hard when they do work, and they work willingly. They have no sordid, selfish, money-getting ways, but rather a fine disdain for mere cash" (*S*, 469). What looks from a distance like shiftlessness is an effect of specific economic conditions. Du Bois elaborates his description of these two fellows by delineating the problems of the crop lien and sharecropping systems, and by noting the ill effects upon the populace of "absentee landlordism" and drastic declines in cotton prices (*S*, 471). Poverty and apparent laziness are the result of deep structural problems. Moreover, in their own way, the two black workers were critics of the Gilded Age, refusing to rouse themselves merely for the purpose of material profit.

In *The American Scene*, however, Du Bois's warning and explanations, which appear in one of the chapters that William singled out for Henry's attention, seem to fall on deaf if not rebellious ears. Traveling through an impoverished Southern landscape on his way to Charleston, James, from his relatively comfortable Pullman, asserts contra Du Bois that "the social scene might be sufficiently penetrated, no doubt from the car window" (*A*, 397). Having eschewed the statistical methods of social scientists and having wedded himself to an impressionistic analysis, James might have assumed, if he assumed anything at all, that Du Bois's censure of "car-window sociologists" was not meant for his "restless analyst." The writer of *The American Scene* is certainly not a sociologist; "reports, surveys and blue-books" are insufficient to capture the qualities that James wishes to record. But whatever the reason, James, in somewhat uneasy disregard of Du Bois's warning, works his rather distant impressions assiduously, and the theme that emerges from these observations is the carelessness of Southern society: "I seem to remember . . . the number of things not cared for" (*A,* 397).

Seeking to account for these "things," James embarks on an analysis that, unlike Du Bois's, attempts to downplay economic analysis. Instead James begins by comparing the scene to a "'short story' in one of the slangy dialects promoted by the illustrated monthly magazines" (*A,* 397), arraigning the Charleston landscape on its lack of taste and aesthetic appeal. When James seeks to figure in his own point of view, however, economic differences return with a vengeance. Commenting on all of the interests that were missing from the Southern story, James remarks that

> the grimness with which, as by a hard inexorable fate, so many things were ruled out, fixed itself most perhaps as the impression of the spectator enjoying from his supreme seat of ease his extraordinary, his awful modern privilege of this detached yet concentrated stare at the misery of subject populations. (Subject, I mean, to this superiority of his bought convenience—subject even as never, of old, to the sway of satraps or proconsuls.) If the subject populations on the road to Charleston, seemingly weak indeed in numbers and in energy, had to be viewed, at all events, so vividly, as not "caring," one made out quite with eagerness that it was because they naturally couldn't. The negroes were more numerous than the whites, but still there *were* whites—of aspect so forlorn and depressed for the most part as to deprecate, though not cynically, only quite tragically, any imputation of value. It was a monstrous thing, doubtless, to sit there in a cushioned and kitchened Pullman and deny to so many groups of one's fellow-creatures any claim to a "personality" but this was in truth what one was perpetually doing. The negroes, though superficially and doubtless not at all intendingly sinister, were the

lustier race; but how could they care (to insist on my point)
for such equivocal embodiments of the right complexion?
Yet these were, practically, within the picture the only af-
firmations of life except themselves; and they obviously, they
notoriously, didn't care for themselves. (A, 397–98)

In this lengthy and convoluted passage James tracks the path from
subjection to subject for the Southern populations within his view
and not only finds the way blocked but also finds that he and the
Pullman in which he is seated are among the major obstacles. The
contrast between the privilege of the Pullman and the poverty of
the countryside is so marked that the social distance between
James and the people he criticizes appears to be greater than that
separating the ruler from the ruled in ancient despotisms. As a passenger on the train—as someone who can pay his way—James is
not merely a spectator but an actor who creates or imputes the values of the scene. In the words of Carolyn Porter, James's acknowledgement of "the seer's complicity without sacrificing his contemplative stance is a concept of action which derives from the identity
of the capitalist and the artist."[7] The necessary aesthetic detach-
ment can be had for the right price, and James can redeem his trip
South only by profiting on his investments.

In addition, having already decided in the chapter on Richmond that the black presence has contributed to the "prison of the
Southern spirit," James cannot but view the numerical dominance
of blacks on the landscape as an impediment to contemplative
ease. The African Americans on the scene are not candidates for
subjectivity in their own right but problems to be overcome or
solved. They are not "intendingly sinister" but presumably sinister
nonetheless—"like some beast that had sprung from the jungle"
(A, 375). On the other hand, what prevents James from imputing
value—the value of subjectivity—to the comparatively few whites
that he sees is their impoverished aspect. They look depressed—as
if they do not care for themselves—and their indifference com-
pounds the problem of black subjectivity. Such subjectivity or caring by African Americans is, for James, theoretically possible;
blacks as servants could care for the whites in their midst. But since
the impoverished whites are such "equivocal embodiments" of
their race, even this mediated path to black caring is interdicted
(A, 398).

All, however, is not lost for James's restless analyst. Having denied others a personality, having decided that his position is part of the problem, James asserts that he "can make up for other deficiencies" by caring enough for all. The aesthetic possibilities of the South might be lost on its natives, but such possibilities will not be lost on James. His receptiveness to impressions will make up the difference.

James's solution is not peculiar to his Southern journey but to his travels taken as a whole. The logic of *The American Scene* dictates that text and author have to make up for what is lacking in the United States. There is, James suggests, an "aesthetic need, in the country, for much greater values, of certain sorts, than the country and its manners, its aspects and arrangements, its past and present, and perhaps even future, really supply" (*A*, 457). James must provide the nation's inhabitants that which they cannot provide themselves. Accordingly, though he seeks those domestic institutions—country clubs, libraries, universities, etc.—that defy the nation's rampant commercialism, he must also deprecate their efficacy, if only to make plain the logic of, and the need for, *The American Scene*. This imputation of national need, perhaps as much as any other factor, may help explain James's treatment of *The Souls of Black Folk* in his text.

Looking upon the extraordinary "vacancy" that comes to characterize Southern life for him, James is brought to wonder, "How can everything so have gone that the only 'Southern' book of any distinction published for many a year is *The Souls of Black Folk*, by that most accomplished of members of the negro race, Mr. W. E. B. Du Bois?" (*A*, 418). With a remarkable backhanded compliment that measures Du Bois's stature against the abnormally stunted growth of the surrounding Southern culture, James attributes Du Bois's prominence as much to the lack of any real competition from other "Southern" writers as to features of the text itself. In doing so, James conveniently overlooks Du Bois's "Northern" upbringing and the possibility that *The Souls of Black Folk* is more a competitor with James's book than with other "Southern" texts. The salience of *The Souls of Black Folk* attests, for James, to the absence of anything else in the American South.

The Souls of Black Folk, of course, was as deeply committed to a critique of the excesses of the Gilded Age as was *The American Scene*. Noting that "all in all, we black men seem the sole oasis of simple faith and reverence in a dusty desert of dollars and smartness" (*S*, 370), Du Bois insisted that the nation could resist the ravages of capitalism only if black Americans embraced ideals rather than wealth. In an extended conceit that amounted to a restaging of Booker T. Washington's Atlanta Exposition speech, which offered a blueprint for black economic growth, Du Bois looked upon the city of Atlanta and wrote, "Here stands this black young Atalanta, girding herself for the race that must be run; and if her eyes be still toward the hills and sky as in the days of old, then we may look for noble running" (*S*, 419). As Robert Stepto has noted, "Atlanta serves in *The Souls* as . . . a battleground wherein Du Bois can struggle with the language and influence of a predecessor."[8] Washington had used the occasion of his speech to reiterate his criticism of basing black colleges on the liberal arts model. In his view those black students who "knew more about Latin and Greek when they left school . . . seemed to know less about life and its conditions." These men and women, he told his auditors, had overlooked "the fact that the masses of us are to live by the production of our hands."[9]

In response Du Bois deliberately employed a classical image to represent the city that was showcased as the apotheosis of the new, industrial, prosperous South. Of course, Du Bois had included in *The Souls of Black Folk* a direct criticism of Washington in the chapter "Of Booker T. Washington and Others," which was one of the few chapters that Du Bois wrote specifically for *The Souls of Black Folk*. This chapter, however, merely made more explicit what was evident elsewhere in the volume: the path of Booker T. Washington was not the proper path for black America.

The derivation of Atlanta from the mythical maiden Atalanta was admittedly forced, but in Du Bois's eyes, "if Atlanta be not named for Atalanta, she ought to have been" (*S*, 416). The story of the maiden, who though capable of outrunning even the fastest young man is captured by Hippomenes because she allows herself to be distracted by the three golden apples that he rolls before her, provided for Du Bois an apt image of the potential of black America if it pursued political and intellectual equality and of the dangers it faced if black folk accepted the program of Washington. In addition, Du Bois's formulation may have been autobiographically tinged. So dazzling was the afterglow of Washington's success at Atlanta that Du Bois had initially become part of the chorus of praise that greeted the Wizard of Tuskegee, penning a note to Washington saying, "Let me heartily congratulate you upon your phenomenal success, at Atlanta—it was a word fitly spoken."[10] And Du Bois was also not entirely above the glitter of the Gilded Age. In his *Dusk of Dawn* autobiography, he conjectured that "had it not been for the race problem early thrust upon me and enveloping me, I should have probably been an unquestioning worshiper at the shrine of the social order and economic development into which I was born."[11] "Race," or at least "the race problem," provided a platform for social heterodoxy. Rather than being simply an accident of birth, race becomes a central player in underwriting Du Bois's critique of America. Similar to expatriation, racial alienation provided blacks with the critical distance that made them, to use James's words, simultaneously "as 'fresh' as an inquiring stranger" and "as acute as an initiated native" (*A*, n.p.). The virtues of racial difference in both *The Souls of Black Folk* and *Dusk of Dawn*, however, seemed to issue not only from the specific social and historical conditions of African Americans but also from romantic racial notions of the special qualities possessed by black people. If blacks were to "save" America they would as a group have to cultivate those unique qualities that only they could contribute to the world.

Du Bois worried, though, that even within the black world the "question of cash and a lust for gold" had already largely displaced the values of faith and reverence, and that America would be the worse for that loss. He asked aloud, "What if to the Mammonism of America be added the rising Mammonism of the re-born South, and the Mammonism of this South be reinforced by the budding Mammonism of its half-awakened black millions? Whither, then, is the new-world quest of Goodness and Beauty and Truth gone glimmering?" (*S*, 419). Rather than a dissent from the dominant values of the age, black American life was on the way to becoming an endorsement of the gospel of greed.

Within Du Bois's various reflections on black Americans at the turn of the century, then, were shifting perspectives which were shared by some of his contemporaries. On the one hand, blackness entailed a posture of dissent from or resistance to Gilded Age America; the souls of black folk were a potential remedy for those ills. Howells's Dr. Olney, in *An Imperative Duty*, stood among those articulating this view. Olney saw in blacks a natural "bulwark against the proletarianization of the lower classes" and a counterpoint to what he saw as the public licentiousness of Irish and other immigrants.[12] Somewhat carried away on wave of racial goodwill, Olney speculates at one point that "if the negroes ever have their turn—and if the meek are to inherit the earth they must come to it—we shall have a civilization of such sweetness and goodwill as the world has never known yet. Perhaps we shall have to wait their turn for any real Christian civilization."[13] This romanticized picture of black Americans was as much a product of white misgivings about the changing industrial order as anything else. Although there is some irony in Howells's presentation of Olney's sentiments, the novel does attempt to make Olney's views compatible with a liberal progressive view of race relations. American society could profit from a more general integration of African Americans.

Romanticized views of blacks, however, could also serve the needs of political and social conservatives who wished to discredit or roll back civil rights gains. The happy-go-lucky darky images of the antebellum South could be contrasted favorably to the images of impoverished, potentially dangerous blacks of post-Reconstruction. Such contrasts were staples of plantation fiction and minstrelsy, both of which were going strong through the 1890s. The needs fulfilled by these images were not solely racial: "For many white audiences the black African was the creature of a pre-industrial life style with a pre-industrial appetite,"[14] allowing whites to indulge their nostalgia for a lifestyle that was no longer available to them as they congregated in urban centers. The promise of black America was an assurance that old ways and old pleasures were recuperable.

Of course the old ways were beyond recovery. The solace embodied in popular representations of black Americans could only clash with reality in such a way that the contemporary condition of black folk seemed to be a betrayal of vanishing ideals as well as an index and intensification of the ills of American society. In the black world, Du Bois observed, "changes so curiously parallel to that of the Other-world" were occurring so that "well-paid porters and artisans" were displacing the preachers and teachers who once advocated black ideals (S, 418). African America was as vulnerable to the new commercial industrial order as was the rest of America. Because the emancipation of black Americans and the acceleration of capitalist transformation were roughly coincident it was also possible to see black Americans as somehow responsible for undesirable changes, which accounts in part for the unflattering picture of black America that James drew in *The American Scene*.

II

In many respects, James's preconceptions on his southward journey were all but indistinguishable from plantation romances or minstrel shows—in fact they probably derived from the latter. "One had remembered," James recalled in *The American Scene*, "the old Southern tradition, the house alive with the scramble of young darkies for the honour of fetching and carrying" (*A*, 423), and it was this image that he had hoped to find. What perhaps had made this memory concrete was the combination of the minstrel shows and afterpieces that James had no doubt seen as a child and his brief experience with the young slave boy, Davy, who had come North with his Aunt Sylvia as servants for the Norcom family, and who subsequently escaped. The boy and his mother, in James's words "had been born and kept in slavery of the most approved pattern and such as this intensity of their condition made them a joy, a joy to the curious mind, to consort with." Davy, for James, stood out because "servitude in the absolute thus did more for him socially than we had ever seen done, above stairs or below, for victims of its lighter forms."[15] Although the escape of Sylvia and Davy should have served as a critique of his romanticizations, the picturesque memory of Davy and of the Old South seemed to help keep alive in James the possibility of an alternative to the raw and slovenly society that he excoriated on his Northern and Southern travels.

In *The American Scene* this preferred alternative was not initially the slave South per se. Slavery, James recognized, had been a "monomania" (*A*, 419) and was responsible for all the South's current ills. It was the "interest" that had banished all other interests. Instead of the slave South, the southern past in which James sought "to take refuge" was "the larger, the less vitiated past that had closed a quarter of a century or so before the War, before the fatal time when the South, monomaniacal at the parting of the ways, 'elected' for extension and conquest" (*A*, 418). Though the historical period to which James refers is one that had already fixed itself along lines of white racial dominance, it was, for James a period when other points of view, even the possibility of abolition, could find expression in the South. This South puts in a momentary appearance in Charleston when an "elderly mulatress," whom James takes to be a servant, responds to his knock on the door of an old house, and exposes to him a momentary glimpse "of the vanished order" in the faded, yet picturesque interior (*A*, 403). In the short interval between the woman's opening and closing the door there is a notably brief but conscious interaction between her and James. She knows, or at least James imputes to her, the knowledge that he is seeking some vision of that distant Southern past. Aware that the scene behind her is but a shabby reminder of what had been, she cares enough to feel embarrassed, and, as James says, "before I could see more, and that I might not sound the secret of shy misfortune, of faded pretension, to shut the door in my face" (*A*, 403).

This brief encounter, coupled with his inadvertent entry into a walled garden, having a "finer feeling for the enclosure," a sense of privacy, effects for a time a transfer of James's allegiances from North to South. "One sacrificed the North" in favor of a South where "those aspects in which the consequences of the great folly [slavery] were, for extent and gravity, still traceable; I was cold-bloodedly to prefer them" (*A*, 404). Contrary to his initial impressions, slavery seems not to have banished all interests but to have permitted the possibility of caring. Though James admits that such a change on his part is "monstrous," he cannot help but prefer the picturesque remnant of a slave past to the depressing vacancy he saw on the road to Charleston. Faced with choosing between the two contrasting visions, he wonders, "What in the world was one candidly to do?" (*A*, 405). Thus compelled to choose the slave past, James then entertains the prospect of seeing more of the favorable vision he had met in Charleston. This anticipation attends his journey further South, but it is an anticipation that is not to be fulfilled. He finds during his subsequent encounters with Southern blacks no incident of personal service equal to that quick shutting of the door by the woman in Charleston.

Du Bois, in *The Souls of Black Folk*, had warned his reader not to expect to find "the faithful, courteous slave of other days, with his incorruptible honesty and dignified humility . . . [who] is passing away just as surely as the old type of Southern gentleman is passing" (*S*, 418). The South of the plantation school, if it had ever existed, was no longer to be found.[16] Du Bois had also warned that the confrontation with black Southern poverty could be dis-

concerting; "One can easily see how a person who saw slavery thus
from his father's parlors, and sees freedom on the streets of a
great city, fails to grasp or comprehend the whole of the new picture" (S, 477). Despite this warning, James nonetheless expresses
surprise at what he terms "the apparently deep-seated inaptitude
of the negro race at large for any alertness of personal service"
(A, 423). What prompts James to disparage black servants is an
incident in which a "negro porter . . . put straight down into the
mud of the road the dressing-bag I was obliged, a few minutes latter . . . to nurse on my knees" (A, 423). Thus discomfited by his
muddy trousers, James proceeds to revise his recent transfer of allegiance to the slave order:

> One had counted, with some eagerness, in moving south-
> ward, on the virtual opposite—on finding this deficiency [of
> alert personal service], encountered right and left at the
> North, beautifully corrected; one had remembered the old
> Southern tradition, the house alive with the scramble of
> young darkies for the honour of fetching and carrying; and
> one was to recognize, no doubt, at the worst, its melancholy
> ghost. Its very ghost, however, by my impression had ceased
> to walk; or, if this be not the case, the old planters, the cotton
> gentry, were the people in the world the worst ministered to.
> I could have shed tears for them at moments, reflecting that
> it was for *this* that they had fought and fallen. (A, 423)

As Donna Przybylowicz observes, James's reading of the scene
made him "blind to the possible resentment of the blacks whose re-
luctance to place themselves in a subservient position is deliberate
and not due to any particular lack."[17] The potential politics of
these servants' actions is hidden from his view. But James's blind-
ness is not surprising because the path to black subjectivity in *The
American Scene* runs through their capacity for personal service.
While James can imagine and articulate appeals for understanding
from the Southern "drummer" and the American girl, he makes
no similar attempt on behalf of black servants. From his point of
view, the interpretive options for reading the behavior of black servants are limited: Either the comforting past which he thought he
had glimpsed in Charleston has been thoroughly obliterated, or
quite possibly it had never existed. If the latter is true, then the

Southern planters are confirmed in their folly, for the order they fought to preserve was no different, at least in its aesthetic appeal, from the industrial North.

As he lay to rest the ghost of the plantation "darky," James was busy constructing another black phantasm to take its place. As an index of a South that never was, and an earlier American sense of ease that never really had a chance, figures in black became for James one of the symbols of America's failure to develop any real critical or aesthetic sense. If blacks had not given the Southern planter any sense of aesthetic ease, they gave the current scene its air of disease. James continues his disparagement of black servants by observing that

> the negro waiter at the hotel is in general, by an oddity of his disposition, so zealous to break for you two or three eggs into a tumbler, or to drop for you three or four lumps of sugar into a coffee-cup, that he scarce waits, in either case, for your leave; but these struck me everywhere as the limit of his accomplishment. He lends himself sufficiently to the rough, gregarious bustle of crowded feeding-places, but seemed to fall below the occasion on any appeal to his individual promptitude. (A, 423–24)

Somewhat reminiscent of Louis Leverett in "The Point of View," James finds African Americans ideally suited for, and perhaps emblems of the vulgarity of, American public life. While this view is a direct result of his Southern experience, it seems in the text to start well back of it. James's slightly patronizing but on the whole laudatory view of the old society at Newport, Rhode Island, turns on a black/white dichotomy that, while not explicitly racial, helps underwrite a racial logic. Newport is fondly remembered in *Notes of a Son and Brother* for its leisure, its aesthetic intensity, and its role as a sort of way station for repatriated Americans.[18] In *The American Scene* James celebrated this "handful of mild, oh delightfully mild, cosmopolites" for similar reasons: "their having for the most part more or less lived in Europe, that of their sacrificing openly to the ivory idol whose name is leisure, and that, not least of a formed critical habit" (A, 222). Europe, leisure, and criticism had marked the members of this society as different from those Americans for whom travel was merely tourism, a brief respite from commercial pursuits. Though his tone in describing the old

Newport types is slightly deprecatory—they "move about, vaguely and helplessly, with the shaft [of Europe] still in [their] side" (*A,* 223)—James cannot dismiss them because they stand out as "excrescences on the American surface, where nobody ever criticized, especially after the grand tour, and where *the great black ebony god* of business was the only one recognized" (*A,* 222; emphasis added).

Opposing Newport to the rest of America, spiritual expatriation to tourism, and criticism to bland acceptance, James figures these oppositions in an ivory/ebony contrast. Certainly the concentration of African Americans within the ranks of domestics, particularly the use of blacks as Pullman porters, in conjunction with James's dissatisfaction with American servants, and his hostility to modern travel in general, would have made this association understandable. Du Bois and Washington each, albeit in slightly different ways, link railroad porters to the vitiation of black life. Moreover, the connection of blacks to the vulgarization of civilized behavior had occurred in James's fiction at least since "The Point of View." But the dynamic of *The American Scene* is as much compositional as it is sociological, and the questions of black against white or text against margin were provisional strategies for trying to organize his American impressions—impressions which, detractors of *The American Scene* might insist, were not coherently organized until James wrote "The Jolly Corner," which was published in 1908.

James's lengthy short story, which appeared first in the *English Review* and was quickly revised for the New York Edition of James's work, relates the experiences of fifty-six-year-old Spencer Brydon, whose return to New York after a lengthy absence that mirrors James's own. His return, like his creator's, confronts him with a homeland he know longer knows, and which challenges him to give forth his impressions. But rather than have his protagonist focus on giving an account of the confusing changes in his homeland, James has Brydon admit that his "'thoughts would still be almost altogether about something that concerns only myself.'" Recognizing, perhaps that the subject of *The American Scene* was not so much America but himself, James, through Brydon, allows that subject to center his tale so that the focus becomes "what he might have been, how he might have led his life, and 'turned out,' if he had not so, at the outset, given [New York] up." Fueling these speculations for Brydon is his discovery, while supervising the conversion of one of his houses into apartment units, that despite having opted for an aesthetic life three decades ago, he has "a capacity for business and a sense for construction."[19] This belated discovery becomes so powerful as a possible missed opportunity that Brydon's desire to envision himself as he might have been takes palpable shape. The story finds Brydon, in the house of his birth, the house on the "jolly corner," stalking this alter ego, a figure his friend Alice Staverton claims has appeared in a dream.

James's story exhibits the various oppositions discussed earlier—for example, the "dollars" of New York are counterpointed by an incalculable aesthetic experience, represented by Miss Staverton. Though residing in New York throughout Brydon's absence, Alice nonetheless embodies for Brydon "*their* common, their quite faraway and antediluvian social period and order" (J, 439). The quiet of private life she is able to preserve is played off New York's "public concussions"; and Brydon, who has been away "worshipping strange gods" (J, 450) now speculates about what he would have become had he offered a sacrifice at some domestic shrine. Brydon's private speculations share, in many respects, the depth and dimension of the copious travel narrative James had already composed. This being said, however, what is also intrinsic to "The Jolly Corner" is its patent absurdity and ridiculousness. Investing his search for his alter ego with all the emotional edge of a big-game hunt, Brydon must nonetheless admit that "he might, for a spectator, have figured some solemn simpleton playing at hide-and-seek" (J, 459). His "jungle," the servants' rooms; his prey, the fearful imaginings of his Irish housekeeper—Brydon's drama could be played out on some comic stage. In fact, when after "a calculated absence of three nights" from his stalkings he feels himself being followed, he adopts a strategy of turning around abruptly to see if his alter ego might betray itself:

> He wheeled about, retracing his steps, as if he might so catch in his face at least the stirred air of some other quick revolution. It was indeed true that his fully dislocalised thought of these manoeuveres recalled to him Pantaloon, at the Christmas farce, buffeted and tricked from behind by ubiquitous Harlequin; but it left intact the influence of the conditions

themselves each time he was re-exposed to them, so that in
fact this association, had he suffered it to become constant,
would on a certain side have but ministered to his intenser
gravity. (J, 460)

Similar to the American stage of the period where high drama and
farce cohabited in a way that did not appear incongruous, Brydon's reflections on his antics do not entirely banish the farcical
interpretation. On the contrary, inasmuch as his more serious interpretation of his action persists despite the absurd overtones,
Brydon remains convinced of the gravity of his quest.

As a youthful devotee of American theater, James had ample experience counterbalancing seriousness and farce as part of his aesthetic. "Young Henry was taken to all the leading New York thea-
tres of the mid-century—Burton's, the Broadway, and the
National, Wallack's Lyceum, Niblo's Gardens and Barnum's 'Lecture Room' attached to the Great American Museum."[20] Har-
lequinades were a staple of the stage—farces and burlesques,
which often featured blackface characters. At one point "Negro
specialties were featured on almost every playbill"[21] as afterpieces,
and Christmas traditions included visits to minstrel shows like
"Harlequin Jim Crow" and "The Magic Mustard Pot."[22] In *A Small
Boy and Others* James specifically recalls attending in London "a
Christmas production preluding to the immemorial har-
lequinade," an experience that had been presaged by his many visits to Niblo's Gardens in New York, where, like other New York
theaters, minstrel afterpieces were regularly staged, and where,
James recalled, "we had . . . harlequin and columbine, albeit of less
pure a tradition."[23] In addition, James's *Autobiography* indicates
that the figure of the harlequin provided him an apt metaphor for
presenting the elder Henry James's attitudes towards his sons'
search for a vocation. James's father's willingness to tolerate mean-
derings and changes of mind struck his son as a "happy har-
lequinade."[24]

In alluding to harlequins (whose traditional costume includes
black and white mask and clothing) in "The Jolly Corner," which
is staged appropriately on the "black-and-white squares" of the
floor of Brydon's ancestral home, James casts the aesthetic/com-
mercial dichotomy on which the story turns in a slightly different
light than is commonly assumed. Brydon's facility at handling his

business concerns and the renovation of his other house lead Alice Staverton to conjecture that "if he had but stayed at home he would have anticipated the inventor of the sky scraper. If he had but stayed at home he would have discovered his genius in time really to start some new variety of awful architectural hare and run it till it burrowed in a gold-mine." (J, 440–41). Brydon's alter ego's lack of taste and his pursuit of money would have been figured in his designing of architectural grotesques. But the surprise and shock that attend Brydon's confrontation with the figure he confronts downstairs indicate that what he finds is not what he expects. The face he sees "was unknown, inconceivable, awful, disconnected from any possibility" (J, 474). What he finds is "a black stranger" with white hands on which two fingers are missing.

Brydon is convinced of and appalled by the lack of identity between himself and the black stranger—"Such an identity fitted his at *no* point" (J, 477)—and the shock leads to what he asserts is his death: "Yes—I can only have died" (J, 480). As to the lack of identity between Spencer and the phantom he confronts, however, Alice Staverton, asserts the opposite. Not only is the stranger in some way Spencer, but according to Alice, Spencer himself had, on the morning of the latter's adventure, appeared to her as "a black stranger" (J, 484)—a figure perhaps in blackface. But instead of precipitating a death, whether figurative or literal, this figure performs the office of a cupid, bringing together Alice and Spencer so that the story ends with a mutual declaration of love.

Spencer's alter ego does correspond to Brydon's expectations in terms of wealth (Brydon surmises that his alter ego has a "million a year"), cementing again the connection between black figures on the one had and public vulgarity and commercial interests on the other. Perhaps undergirding this story is not so much a contrast between aesthetics and business but the unsettling territory in which the two meet. Not only is Brydon's European freedom, as Alice astutely notes, made possible by the income derived from his American rents, but James in invoking images from the popular theater also seems to point up another disturbing possibility. The aesthetic alternative for a figure like Brydon or James would not have been to construct monstrous but impressive skyscrapers but to become a participant in the production of "'intellectual' pabulum" to fulfill the democratic demand—a demand so great that "the journalist, the novelist, the dramatist, the genealogist, the historian, are pressed as well, for dear life, into the service" (A, 458). Among the available options was participation on the minstrel stage. As Alexander Saxton points out, "typical purveyors of minstrelsy, then, were northern and urban; they were neither New Englanders nor Southerners (although their parents may have been); and if of rural or small town origin, were most likely to have come from upper New York State." Like James they were "eager to break into the exclusive and inhospitable precincts of big city theater."[25]

James clearly associated writing for the theater with the "thought of fabulous fortunes," worldly success, and aesthetic disfigurement—his plays were, in his words, "mutilated" and "massacred," not unlike the maimed figure Brydon meets in "The Jolly Corner." Writing for the theater was a form of devil worship, "a most unholy trade." And though James's major theatrical debacle, the production of *Guy Domville*, took place on the British stage, his desire for success as a dramatist, was quite possibly a species of "the strong American impulse that he no doubt possessed . . . to elbow one's way to achievement by solid worldly enterprise!"[26] In a possible pun on *Guy Domville*, Spencer describes his unfitness to play his alter ego's role by saying that he couldn't have worn his monocle in the stranger's environment: "I couldn't have sported mine 'downtown.' They'd have guyed me there" (J, 485). Moreover, inasmuch as minstrelsy continued to appear on the British stage through the turn of the century, the market in which James would have imagined himself a competitor would have featured blackface performers as well.

The remedy for James's problem was not a purge of the theater so to speak, but a habit of critical distinction. As we saw earlier, James's recollections of his childhood visits to the theater stressed his growth as a young critic, as someone who could make the proper distinctions. In "The Jolly Corner," where the possibility of seeing Spencer Brydon as a ridiculous figure, where the possibility of "guying" him is openly acknowledged, Alice Staverton, whose "imagination would still do him justice," provides the necessary discerning audience. Unlike the London audience which mercilessly condemned James's enactment of the conflict between two contradictory modes of life, Staverton's ironic comments and criticisms are "not, like the cheap sarcasms with which one heard most people, about the world of 'society,' bid for the reputation of cleverness, from nobody's really having any" (J, 444). She can appreciate both the black stranger and Brydon's difference from him; she can accept and appreciate both.

The point here, however, is not so much that "The Jolly Corner" is directly about James's thwarted theatrical desires. Rather I want to stress that over the course of the 1880s, 1890s, and through the turn of the century, popular representations of black/white racial difference exert a constant pressure on the work of an author like James such that in thinking through the possibility of aesthetic redemption it seemed almost necessary to distance oneself from black strangers. By masking Brydon's other self in black, "The Jolly Corner," like black minstrelsy, simultaneously acknowledged the power of, while establishing the means of control over, the Other.

The pity and acceptance that Alice Staverton in feels towards the black stranger dissipate in her relief that Brydon and not the stranger is the figure whose head rests on her lap. After having asserted an identity between Spencer and the black stranger, she recants and assures Brydon in the story's final sentence that "he isn't—no, he isn't—*you!*" (J, 485)—thus distancing Brydon and herself from the vulgarities of a New York in which the house on the jolly corner will seemingly function as an ironic oasis.

Alice Staverton's assurance to Brydon that he is not a part of the ravaged life that surrounds them is an assurance that many realists, confronted with the unsettling social changes brought about by immigration, economic upheaval, conservative backlash against progressive reform, as well as their own attacks on convention and tradition, could not themselves feel. Americans at the close of the nineteenth century found themselves in what Lawrence Levine calls "a universe of strangers," strangers who "spilled over into the public spaces that characterized nineteenth-century America and that included theaters, music halls, opera houses, museums, parks, fairs, and the rich public cultural life that took place daily on the streets of American cities." For elites like James, culture, in the sense of high culture, became a place of refuge, a place of "retreat."[27] Despite the fact that African-American access to these places, and to "culture" itself was often limited by statutory, economic, and even aesthetic factors, the black presence was never entirely absent. As attested to by the minstrel echoes in "The Jolly Corner," in the American context, "culture" could never be a comfortable refuge. Writers like Henry James were always confronting and seeking to contain their own participation in and complicity with the aspects of their society they deplored. It is within these efforts to define and distinguish among the values of American cultural life that it becomes possible to trace the racial dimensions of the American literary imagination.

CONCLUSION

In many respects the volatility and sense of danger attending the recognition of aesthetic identities across the color line have not abated appreciably since the turn of the century. The now infamous critical exchange between Joyce A. Joyce on one side, and Houston Baker and Henry Louis Gates, Jr., on the other, which took place on the pages of *New Literary History,* is a case in point. Joyce charged that by applying academic literary theory to the study of black texts her two male colleagues were making African-American literary criticism more responsive to the interests of white institutions than to the interests of blacks themselves. Maintaining that African-American post-structuralists had forgotten their responsibility "to affect, to guide, to animate, and to arouse the minds and emotions of Black people," Joyce viewed these critics as having gone off to worship strange gods.[1] Predictably, Gates and Baker denied Joyce's accusation in terms equally generous, but their responses, and Joyce's counter, hardly settled the matter.[2] The simultaneous demands of institutional responsibility and racial loyalites are so convoluted that in one way or another perhaps every black critic of African-American literature—and some white scholars as well—has been drawn into the orbit of this argument.[3]

I invoke the debate here not so much in hopes of settling it (though I suppose one can always hope) but primarily because the substance of Joyce's charge against her male counterparts is also the substance of the charge that Baker, in *Workings of the Spirit,* makes against Frances Harper's *Iola Leroy.* Harper's novel, according to Baker, "is an essentially conservative appeal to white public opinion" and is out of touch with the black masses. Harper and her turn-of-the-century compeers, Pauline Hopkins and Anna Julia Cooper, are prodigal daughters who have "departed" from their black cultural roots, casting their lot with "a bright Victorian morality in whiteface."[4]

That Joyce's charge against Baker and that Baker's charge against early black women novelists and critics are virtually the same suggests that this conflict over which aesthetic and critical practices best serve the interest of the black masses may point to a larger structural problem. As Theodore Mason observes in his assessment of the debate, "If we step outside the upper-class circle of higher education and ask the question, who reads any serious literature or literary comment (even a Baldwin essay in *Essence*), the frightening answer to that question should be enough to damage the position which advocates conferring authority on a populist audience."[5] Neither position can make good a claim to mass political representation.

Appropriately, perhaps, Harper's *Iola Leroy* anticipated some of Mason's misgivings about literary populism. The novel offers a rather pessimistic observation about the potential for literary consumption in the Southern rural economy. Despite its relative popular success, Harper's text suggests that the bourgeois motivations for reading—companionship, leisure activity, spiritual comfort—are determined by the material circumstances of a particular class. When the genteel Robert Johnson asks Aunt Linda whether she has learned to read yet, the following discussion ensues:

> "No, chile, sence freedom's com'd I'se bin scratchin' too hard to get a libin' to put my head down to de book."
>
> "But, Aunt Linda, it would be such company when your husband is away, to take a book. Do you never get lonesome?"
>
> "Chile, I ain't got no time ter get lonesome. Ef you had eber so many chickens to feed, an' pigs squealin' fer somethin' ter eat, an' yore ducks an' gees squakin' 'roun' yer, yer wouldn't hab time ter git lonesome."
>
> "But, Aunt Linda, you might be sick for months, and think what a comfort it would be if you could read your Bible."
>
> "Oh, I could hab prayin' and singin'. Dese people is mighty good 'bout prayin' by de sick. Why, Robby, I think it would gib me de hysterics ef I war to try to git book larnin' froo my pore ole head." (*I,* 156)

"Praying" and "singing" are the expressive forms that seem to make sense for Aunt Linda's situation, and though she also blames herself for being unable to read, she has already made apparent the material realities that prevent her from putting her "head down to de book." Linda does admit that she "likes to yere dem dat can" read, but as the narrator puts it, "Aunt Linda was kind and obliging, but there was one place where she drew the line, and that was at learning to read" (*I*, 276). To be sure, education and uplift of the Southern freedman is the recurring theme of Harper's novel, and the quest for literacy is palpable, especially with the younger generation. Sprinkled throughout the text, however, are admissions like those made by another elderly character that "ef yer wants to put me to sleep jis' put a book in my han'" (*I*, 171).

It is clear to Harper that the black race can readily provide the stuff of literature: "There is material among us for the broadest comedies and the deepest tragedies" (*I*, 262). But as she attempts to imagine how novel reading might become integral to the daily practices of black folk, not only does she find that the material conditions of black southern life appear to conspire against her, but that the spiritual forms of black expressive culture—praying and singing—seem to obviate the need for novel reading. Comfort and consolation can be found in oral expressive forms, making even Bible reading superfluous. At the same time, the secular haunts, the "dens of vice" that would be so nuturing for the blues and jazz, are anathema to Harper's message of temperance. Thus Harper's novel, which imagines itself as being of "lasting service to the race," also emerges as an expressive form in competition and conflict not only with other means of black expression but with the very material circumstances that generate those forms of expression.

To place the matter in this light is to suggest that Baker is correct in seeing the intersection between the late nineteenth-century African-American women's novel as a form and African-American culture as a whole as a point of conflict rather than of harmony. But it is also to suggest that Harper herself was well aware of the problem. Harper's novel, in Baker's terms, looms on the black cultural horizon as an alien form whose conventions and representational strategies estrange it from "a nineteenth-century black women's vernacular southern culture in the heroism of its economic survival, and then in the resonances of its quilts, gardens, conjuration, supper-getting-ready songs, churched melodies, woven baskets of Charleston wharves, and culinary magnificence."[6]

It is this estrangement that vernacular-based canonical critiques of African-American literature have sought to heal with the belief that by bringing to bear the "virtues of the vernacular," African-American novelists (and by extension, critics) could locate their texts "at the locus of the black neighborhood, the maternal home front, or the southern vernacular community." Powered by the assumption that the goal of black textual practice is to resituate black literary and critical texts within a canonical tradition whose dimensions are rhetorical, aesthetic, and even spiritual, black vernacular criticism like that practiced by Baker can find little of value in books like Harper's *Iola Leroy,* whose use of Victorian norms to suture the black peasantry to the black bourgeoisie accords vernacular characters a treatment too much like that they receive in the pages of white-authored fiction. Thus, in assessing *Iola Leroy,* Baker seems almost astonished at what he finds: "we view its endless pages of exposition and lofty sentiment—its creakingly mechanical and entirely predictable plot—with a kind of detached wonder, knowing that its author was both abolitionist lecturer and journeyer in the South. And we can only grasp the 'behold the star' quality of the text and not quite believe in it."[7] Baker's rather belletristic assessment of Harper's novel makes evident his sense of dislocation. Seeking to reconcile the activist with the novelist, Baker looks upon the latter and all but repeats the words of Iola Leroy's brother after they reunite: "You are so changed I do not think I would have known you if I had met you in the street!" (*I,* 195). As if confronting a phantom—a black text in "whiteface"—Baker's vernacular practice regards *Iola Leroy* as little more than a white stranger within the black tradition. Despite its central character's condemnation of those figures who would commit treason against the race, Harper's novel becomes a prodigal daughter, almost unrecognizable to its own black "family."

More troublingly, Baker sees Harper's problem as representative of the contemporary critical practice of many black academic women. "The desire of Afro-American women critics who comprise today's historical majority is not unlike that of the turn-of-the-century Afro-American daughters who sought to incorporate themselves into an essentialist, northern, history."[8] Though it is tempting to treat Baker's criticism of the majority of African-American women critics as idiosyncratic, I will, perhaps willfully, view it as symptomatic of a larger problem within the practice of canonical/ vernacular/ blues theorizing that, despite significant variations, links Baker with Gates and critics like Michael Awkward (and, not so ironically, with some of the scholars Baker censures). My point here is not that these other critics necessarily share Baker's assessment of contemporary black women critics but that they are in basic agreement about what is at stake in defining African-American literary critical practice. (Conversely, as illustrated by Diana Fuss's *Essentially Speaking*, it is possible to agree with Baker's general characterization of contemporary African-American criticism by black women—"With the exception of the recent work of Hazel Carby and Hortense Spillers, black feminist critics have been reluctant to renounce essentialist critical positions and humanist literary practices."[9]—without endorsing fully the project of vernacular critique. Despite the variations and nuances among the vernacular critics, there is common to them a sense that at risk in African-American literary critical practice is the individual critic's racial identity or integrity.[10] To be sure, Baker, Gates, and Awkward have all levied criticisms against those who seek to identify a critic's race with her politics; and each has questioned the charges of racial treason that certain scholars have sought to bring against their black colleagues with whom they have intellectual disagreements. Nonetheless, what we find in their works is the stern warning that the black scholar, faced with an array of critical methods and practices, must proceed carefully, for she is in ever-present danger of becoming an ideologically white Other: "a faint echo of her master's voice," a "talking android," or a writer of texts "indistinguishable from other texts in the Western literary tradition."[11] Not only does aesthetic practice become a matter of locating and celebrating the "black difference," but resisting or exposing "white hegemony" requires that one cling to that same difference.[12]

In a political environment where intellectual and political conservatives, under the guise of championing "color-blindness" and "universalism," have proceeded to discredit all challenges to the status quo as antidemocratic, elitist, and barbaric, it is easy to see why one would not want to yield too readily the politics of difference. To give up the particularity of individual and specific group histories would seem to leave one with no possibility of resisting the steamroller of current hegemonic practices. The point, however, as Hazel Carby makes clear, is not to "abandon ideas of cultural difference" and the ways in which those differences have been "antagonistic to cultures of domination."[13] Rather it is to question whether the current articulations of black difference remain tenable as oppositional critical practices; whether they "themselves [have] become so firmly established as to become obstacles to illuminating, 'fresh' interpretations";[14] or whether even the production of "fresh" interpretations is of any political moment.

To take the last point first, Mason's misgivings about literary populism derive from the observation that the reading and writing of literature and literary criticism is "controlled by brute economic and class considerations. . . . [and that] financial considerations determine completely one's capacity to benefit from the collective wisdom of writers and critics."[15] There are, no doubt, produce exceptions to Mason's generalizations, but their general accuracy is undeniable. Literary criticism is a narrowly circumscribed activity (but even so, not entirely powerless). And if the novel, as opposed to the academic criticism it has engendered, has, through the imaginative efforts of the Toni Morrisons, Alice Walkers, and Charles Johnsons, maintained an audience and influence not entirely coincident with the walls of the academy, the comfort one can take in this dissemination would be minimal.

Vernacular critics have attributed the success of contemporary African-American letters to the adeptness of black practitioners at transforming their high-cultural practices into vital transactions through an encounter with traditional vernacular practices, from street language to quilting to cooking to the planting of gardens. In doing so they have generally insisted on a one-way transformation, despite Gates's assertion that the application of post-structuralist theory "changes both the received theory and received ideas about the text."[16] Gates's substitution of "received ideas about the text" for simply "text" is indicative. His work seeks to cushion the shock of his defamiliarizing gesture by claiming that in applying theory to black literature he is doing nothing that black writers themselves have not done for centuries. Likewise for Baker and for Awkward there is, to let Awkward speak for both, a stress on "those appropriative acts by Afro-Americans which have successfully transformed, by the addition of black expressive cultural features, Western cultural and expressive systems to the extent that they reflect, in black 'mouths' and 'contexts,' what we might call (in Bakhtinian terms) Afro-American 'intention' and 'accent.'"[17] But what gets finessed in the invocation of Bakhtinian dialogism is the way the process works in reverse. If the African-American novel and African-American criticism have achieved unprecedented popularity and visibility by apparently responding to the imperatives of a black cultural tradition, the felt need to novelize these other cultural forms as a way of paying them homage attests to sweeping changes occuring within what we deem the black tradition. The novel as a form, Fredric Jameson has observed, plays "a significant role in . . . that immense process of transformation whereby populations whose life habits were formed by other, now archaic, modes of production are effectively reprogrammed for life and work in the new world of market capitalism."[18] Regardless of whether a novel seems at a mimetic or rhetorical level to get at the truth of a black experience and a novelist appears to succeed in "placing her work in the expressive tradition of her people that dates back hundreds, perhaps thousands, of years,"[19] what is also no doubt happening is that the traditional practices that the novel represents or exemplifies are being repackaged for consumption by black and white elites. The problem, in its way, is Jamesian. The American expatriate found that while the ascendance of the novel as a cultural form marked the novelist's centrality as cultural role player, a society that had come to depend on the novel for "culture" could no longer be the society that he had hoped to defend.

Vernacular critics have not been oblivious to this problem, and Baker specifically has tried to counter the charge that "authentic Afro-American particularity has been undermined by the standardizing imperatives of mass capitalism,"[20] Arguing provocatively that "making black expressiveness a commodity . . . is a crucial move in a repertoire of black survival motions in the United States," Baker goes on to suggest that "in Afro-American culture, exchanging words for safety and profit is scarcely an alienating act. It is, instead, a defining act in expressive culture."[21] The black academic critic and the black folk artist are in the same economic boat because both must market their self-expressions. For African Americans the experience of slavery has been decisive. The market and its commodifying effects have always defined the black American experience.

However, even if one were to grant the efficacy of Baker's tactical move as a way of doing away with the problem of the "alienation" of a black bourgeoise from its black folk roots, the tactic would still not help Baker toward his other goal of "locating the

culturally specific in Afro-American life and expression." For
Baker describes the key difference between white and black aesthetic relations to the market as an "affective" one. White artists experience "angst" about their relations to the market in a way not
indicative of black expressive culture. He argues that "Afro-Amer-
ica's exchange power has always been coextensive with its stock of
expressive resources," and that "the angst assumed to accompany
commodity status is greatly alleviated when that status constitutes
a sole means of securing power in a hegemonic system."[22] The
black novelist, critic, or scholar need not worry about commodification—it's inevitable and, in fact, constitutive of black cultural
practice. It serves no purpose to have feelings about that which you
cannot change.

Baker's gambit, however, cannot answer the purpose of cultural
specificity because the affective distinction fails to hold up. From
within Americanist academic literary criticism at large, in the person of Walter Benn Michaels, has come the same message: the
market is coextensive with culture, and "it thus seems wrong to
think of the culture you live in as the object of your affections: you
don't like it or dislike it, you exist in it."[23] In Michaels we find at
least one not-insignificant figure from "outside" blues/vernacular
critique whose criticism of the novelist's "affective response" to
commodification seems little different from that which Baker rec-
ommends for the blues artist. This is not the place to embark upon
a critique of Michaels's work, or to speculate about the possibility
that slavery has made black culture precociously postmodern, but
the similarities between Michaels and Baker at this point are
enough to suggest that what Baker registers as cultural specificity
is merely further exemplification of the career of the commodity
in late capitalism and a peculiarly productive moment in the realm
of academic literary scholarship.[24]

If Baker's attempt to escape the problems attending the vernacular critic's articulation of oppositional black difference ultimately fails, it is precisely, as Adolph Reed observes, because "mo-
nopoly capitalism has entered a new stage typified by the extension
of the administrative apparatus throughout everyday life," and because the terms of black difference aid the rationalization of this
apparatus by functioning as "commodified facsimiles of diversity."
As Reed puts the problem, rather devastatingly, "artificial black
particularity provided the basis for the myth of genuine black com-

munity and consequently legitimated the organization of the black population into an administrative unit—and, therefore, the black elite's claims to primacy."[25] Here Baker's own words seem particularly damning, for the vision of black politics with which he identifies his critical strategies is an openly administrative one—an "Afro-American politics conceived in terms of who gets what and when and how."[26] To be sure, within these specified parameters, what one sees is visible success in the form of changes within, and establishment of, educational institutions, publishing ventures, and the like. The rise of vernacular critique has participated in an enhancement of the prestige of African-American literary scholarship, unprecedented movement of black scholars within the literary profession, and a general increase in the availability of works by and about African Americans. These are real if woefully insufficient gains. And though their correspondence with the political and economic "sacrifice of a growing share of the black population" is not accidental,[27] the capacity of "history" to move in unexpected directions and the necessity of working within what is (for what else is there?), towards what might be, prevents one from being simply dismissive. Nonetheless it seems clear, as various scholars, myself included, have pointed out elsewhere, that as an interpretive and political strategy vernacular critique entails serious liabilities, not the least of which are the depoliticization of black cultural discussion and the tendency to suppress and discredit internal dissent.[28]

But if not a criticism and a politics centered upon the black difference, then what? Sad to say, there is no simple comprehensive answer to that question. *Black and White Strangers* did not proceed with the idea that it would develop a new, African-American critical method which would delineate a set of identifiably black critical operations that other scholars could subsequently apply. To have done so would have been to recreate many of the problems I have discussed in regard to vernacular critical practice. Rather, I proceeded on the assumption that the construction of black/white racial difference in the United States has been so central to our political, imaginative, and economic lives that it ought to be possible to trace the process of this construction in a variety of cultural places, many of them unexpected and not yet adequately examined. The analysis that James makes of the South and slavery in *The American Scene* is applicable to the whole of American life. Com-

menting that "the negro had always been and could absolutely not
fail to be, intensely 'on the nerves' of the South" (A, 376), James
also observed that the South's attempts to control this black omni-
presence through slavery had meant "the eternal bowdlerization
of books and journals; meant in fine all literature and all art on an
expurgatory index. It meant, still further, an active and ardent
propaganda; the reorganization of the school, the college, the university, in the interest of the new criticism" (A, 374). The whole of
the South's literary output, according to James, had been shaped,
dialogized, by the black presence. Wherever one looked one could
not fail to notice the silences, evasions, and distortions marking
that presence. And what the slave order entailed upon Southern
cultural life, the black/white racial order has entailed upon the nation's cultural life as a whole. In order to "see" what has been ex-
purgated and expunged one must, to repeat Toni Morrison's
words, embark upon an "examination and re-interpretation of the
American canon, the founding nineteenth-century works for the
'unspeakable things unspoken'; for the ways in which the presence
of Afro Americans has shaped the choices, the language, the structure—the meaning of so much American literature."[29]
   In following out the ramifications of tracing racial effects
throughout the whole of American cultural life, I also thought I
would investigate another area that contemporary African-American critical practice had largely skirted: the domain of risks and
benefits incurred by an African-Americanist investigation of
"mainstream" aesthetic texts. While texts such as Gates's *Figures in
Black* and *The Signifying Monkey* or Baker's *Blues, Ideology, Afro-American Fiction,* and *Workings of the Spirit* are replete with examples of
documentary, instrumental, and appropriative uses of critical,
theoretical, philosphical, and historical texts by writers who don't
happen to be black, these texts have precious little to say about encounters with white-authored texts as aesthetic objects, as sources
of pleasure, even as they provide objects of ideological critique.[30]
While it was clear to me, for example, that I had to read Thomas
Dixon for scholarly reasons, as a document in the history of American racism, I also had to acknowledge that my reading of much of
James and Howells proceeded both from my desire to chart the
workings of race in late nineteenth-century literary culture as well
as from the fact that, despite their problems, I happened to enjoy
reading many of these novels. What I wondered was whether it was

possible to treat together in a single study how I saw these fictions working for me as well as how I saw them working against me. I'm not sure even now to what degree I sacrificed one set of concerns on behalf of the other. What was clear to me, however, was the assumption implicit within much contemporary African-American critical practice—that one's pleasures were necessarily on all fours with one's politics—could not serve as an effective guide.

But where, ultimately, is the politics in the kind of study I have written? The potential political liabilities are perhaps most obvious. To argue that reading Henry James ought to be central to our study of race might be seen as conceding too much to cultural conservatives who tout the capacity of canonical texts to deal effectively with the entire spectrum of human concerns. Despite having asserted the necessity of reading James in conjunction with Du Bois and Harper, the fact remains that if I have done my job well some of my readers will be prompted to peruse or reperuse some of the mainstream texts I analyze. At a more mundane level, the time spent reading James, which can be considerable, is admittedly time away from the black-authored texts that have been neglected or only recently discovered. These are obviously risks and liabilities, but risks that I'm willing to run for a political payoff that is admittedly "contingent."[31]

Not so very long ago it seemed a sufficiently oppositional gesture to deconstruct the opposition between art and ideology that sustained literary scholarly practice in this country. In responding to high modernism's elevation of art over politics, Left cultural critique found it useful to expose the ideological assumptions of that claim as well as the way that those individual authors and texts deemed universal actually embodied and enacted particular class interests. The power of dominant orders resided in their ability to secure consent surreptitiously in part through their deployment of aesthetics. Against this deployment a necessary counterhegemonic strategy was to reveal the complicity of aesthetics with politics. If disinterest always cloaked particular, specifiable interests, the party of "disinterest" could always be embarrassed by having its interests exposed.

But if nothing else, I hope that the argument in the previous chapters has shown that political and textual strategies always have unexpected outcomes. In this case, the cultural Right, having gotten over its initial embarrassment that its aesthetics could no longer be claimed to be unarguably disinterested, has now readily welcomed the Left's welding of aesthetics and politics. If defending a traditional literary canon is the same as defending free market capitalism, is the same as opposing affirmative action policies, then that is all to the good. By creating a chain of values that links Shakespeare to matters of contemporary conservative policy, the Right has been able to give its policy agenda an aura of cultural and historical authority that creates powerful conservative communities of interest for whom speaking out against multiculturalism and for the "Great Books" is self-evidently equivalent to speaking on behalf of constitutional guarantees of individual freedom, which is self-evidently equivalent to waging war against a Middle Eastern dictator. The apparent obviousness of these equations is such that these spokespersons are exempted from having to articulate the reasons and arguments for the connections being made. Names of canonical writers and phrases like the "Western tradition" become talismans to wave at the cultural infidels on the Left.

By conceding, as does Gates in *The Signifying Monkey,* a vision of white cultural ownership, of a Western tradition that has been "created and borne, in the main, by white men,"[32] one purchases like ownership of the black tradition—"We are the keepers of the black literary tradition."[33] To sanction this exchange, however, is also to allow the Right to deploy one of its most useful fantasies, the idea that the values associated with white masculinity can make contemporary Americans at home in history, can define them as uncontested heirs of the past, as "inheritors of Western civilization."[34] A real history of economic, social, and political domination by white males then becomes simply a story of white cultural curatorship. Consequently, contemporary cultural conservatives can represent themselves, like the young boy in James Joyce's "Araby," as knight errants bearing their "chalices safely through a throng of foes." But unlike Joyce's youthful protagonist they are never brought round to an epiphany that reveals them as "creatures driven and derided by vanity."[35]

Thus, despite the fact that Henry James's twenty-year absence from his homeland led him to regard most of his countrymen as vulgar strangers, and despite the fact of his ultimately having adopted British citizenship, contemporary conservatives can indulge themselves in a fantasy of ahistorical collegiality with "the Master," never having to come to terms with the extent to which they are not merely fellow readers of the texts that James himself enjoyed but also products of and necessarily apologists for the very social order that James found abhorrent. Federal education officials can without any sense of irony tell us that what is wrong with our public schools is that they fail to include in their curricula the very writers who found the idea of public schooling inimical to their sense of society and culture. And newspaper writers can bash university professors in the name of Western culture, blithely ignorant of the fact that for many of the writers they champion the growing prominence of daily journalism all but sounded the death knell for any possibility of a viable American literary culture. The necessary alienation which attends a confrontation with history is described as unhistorical and we are told, in the words of former Secretary of Education William Bennett, that if our students' "past is hidden from them, they will become aliens in their own culture, strangers in their own land."[36]

The admittedly tenuous political payoff in the project I have sketched is to force scholars on the cultural Right to respond to the fact of their own undeniable alienation from the cultural legacy they champion, to recognize the contradictions within their own formulations, to have to answer questions about the hypocrisy of their aims—ultimately to have to explain that which they now simply assert. In recent years conservatives have been able to attack what passes for a Left in our society by pointing up contradictions and problems within Left critique without having to attend to the real problems lying at the heart of their own cultural project. Under the guise of perfect coherence, of a smooth articulation of past and present, the Right is now busy sweeping before it all vestiges of any significant opposition, and doing so in the name of democracy and liberty.[37] As a result, as I write these words, conditions do not seem propitious for a cultural project whose goal is an immediate mobilization of an oppositional Left. But if one can at least force those now hauling the juggernaut of the West to pause, however briefly, in their celebratory procession, there may be time, if for nothing else, to allow some of us at least to get out of the way of its wheels, and then perhaps to think about the next necessary step.

NOTES

INTRODUCTION

1. Quoted in Edmund Wilson, *Patriotic Gore: Studies in the Literature of the American Civil War* (New York: Farrar, Straus, and Giroux, 1962), p. 3.

2. Mark Twain, *Life on the Mississippi,* (New York: New American Library, 1961), p. 266.

3. Twain, *Life on the Mississippi,* p. 276.

4. George Washington Cable, "My Politics," in *The Negro Question: A Selection of Writings on Civil Rights in the South,* ed. Arlin Turner (Garden City, N.Y.: Doubleday and Co., 1958), p. 16. See also Twain, *Life on the Mississippi,* p. 267. Twain also includes Joel Chandler Harris as a Southerner whose style was not Southern.

5. Larzer Ziff, *The American 1890s: Life and Times of a Lost Generation* (Lincoln: University of Nebraska Press, 1966), p. 336.

6. Leo Bersani, *A Future for Astyanax: Character and Desire in Literature* (New York: Columbia University Press, 1984) p. 60–61. I mean for Bersani's book to stand as a synecdoche for a host of other works questioning the oppositional status of realism, including some works which dissent from the full import of Bersani's arguments. Most significant are Catherine Belsey, *Critical Practice* (London: Methuen and Co., 1980); Walter Benn Michaels, *The Gold Standard and the Logic of Naturalism: American Literature at the Turn of the Century* (Berkeley: University of California Press, 1987); Mark Seltzer, *Henry James and the Art of Power* (Ithaca, N.Y.: Cornell University Press, 1984). Although Michaels (see pp. 46–58) and Seltzer (see pp. 15–22) criticize Bersani's formulations, they are essentially in agreement that realism's attempts to oppose society are in one way or another undermined.

7. Bersani, *A Future for Astyanax,* pp. 61–62.

8. Gerald Graff, "American Criticism Left and Right," in *Ideology and Classic American Literature,* ed. Sacvan Bercovitch and Myra Jehlen (New York: Cambridge University Press, 1986), p. 115.

9. Daniel Borus's recent study of realism, which seeks to supplement

New Historical accounts of the period with an analysis that does not shy away from "causation," admits to making "little mention of the two pivotal factors of race and gender." Recognizing that "no complete history of literary discourse in the United States can ignore these two dimensions of both authorship and readership," Borus's argument makes it necessary for him to focus "on the primary and structural relationships into which racial and gender factors ultimately entered" (pp. 9–10). I hope to reveal the role of race in constructing "primary and structural relationships." See Daniel H. Borus, *Writing Realism: Howells, James, and Norris in the Mass Market* (Chapel Hill: University of North Carolina Press, 1989).

10. See Sterling A. Brown, *The Negro in American Fiction* (1937; rpt. New York: Atheneum, 1969), and Alain Locke, "The Saving Grace of Realism: Retrospective Review of the Negro Literature of 1933," *Opportunity* 13 (Jan. 1934): 8–11, rpt. in *The Critical Temper of Alain Locke: A Selection of His Essays on Art and Culture,* ed. Jeffrey C. Stewart (New York: Garland Publishing, Inc., 1983), pp. 221–23

11. Eric Foner, *Reconstruction: America's Unfinished Revolution* (New York: Harper and Row, 1989), p. xxi.

12. Robert A. Bone, *The Negro Novel in America* (New Haven: Yale University Press, 1960), p. 21. Charles Scruggs, in *The Sage of Harlem: H. L. Mencken and the Black Writers of the 1920s* (Baltimore: Johns Hopkins University Press, 1984), similarly dismisses Howells as unimportant to the development of the early African-American novel: "Howells's extra-aesthetic views triumphed over his realist principles and, in retrospect, it seems that Mencken was quite right to ignore him as an important influence upon realism in Negro letters" (p. 185).

13. Albion W. Tourgée, "The South as a Field for Fiction," *The Forum* 6 (Dec. 1888): p. 411.

14. Tourgée refers to his earlier prediction in ibid., p. 404.

15. Ibid., p. 413.

16. Ibid., p. 406.

17. Henry James, letter to John Hay, 13 May 1885, rpt. in James, *The Bostonians,* ed. Alfred Habegger (1886; Indianapolis: Bobbs-Merrill, 1976), p. 436.

18. Leslie A. Fiedler, *Love and Death in the American Novel,* rev. ed (New York: Scarborough Books, 1982), p. 474.

19. Ibid., p. 493 (emphasis added).

20. William Dean Howells, *Editor's Study,* ed. James W. Simpson (Troy, N.Y.: Whitson Publishing Co., 1983), p. 22; this is a facsimile edition of Howells's monthly "Editor's Study" columns from *Harper's Monthly.*

21. See Howells, "Majors and Minors," *Harper's Weekly* (27 June 1896): 630, and "A Psychological Counter-Current in Fiction," *North American Review* 173 (Dec. 1901): 882. Cf. Henry Louis Gates, Jr., *Figures in Black:*

Words, Signs, and the Racial Self (New York: Oxford University Press, 1987), pp. 22–23, and Bernard W. Bell *The Afro-American Novel and Its Tradition* (Amherst: University of Massachusetts Press, 1987), pp. 58–59, on Howells's limitations vis à vis these writers.

22. Gates, *Figures in Black*, p. 45.

23. Gates, "'What's in a Name'?: Some Meanings of Blackness," *Dissent* 36 (1989): 493.

24. Gates, "Canon-Formation and the Afro-American Tradition," in *Afro-American Literary Study in the 1990s*, ed. Houston A. Baker, Jr., and Patricia Redmond (Chicago: University of Chicago Press, 1989), p. 28.

25. Michaels, *The Gold Standard and the Logic of Naturalism*, p. 27.

26. Tourgée, "The South as a Field for Fiction," p. 405.

27. Seltzer, *Henry James and the Art of Power*, p. 154.

28. See Bersani, *A Future for Astyanax*, pp. 59–60.

29. Eric J. Sundquist, "The Country of the Blue," in *American Realism: New Essays*, ed. Sundquist (Baltimore: Johns Hopkins University Press, 1982), p. 20.

30. Michaels, *The Gold Standard and the Logic of Naturalism*, p. 51.

31. See Fredric Jameson, *The Political Unconscious: Narrative as a Socially Symbolic Act* (Ithaca, N.Y.: Cornell University Press, 1981), p. 9.

32. The texts not already cited are June Howard, *Form and History in American Literary Naturalism* (Chapel Hill: University of North Carolina Press, 1985), Amy Kaplan, *The Social Construction of American Realism* (Chicago: University of Chicago Press, 1988), Carolyn Porter, *Seeing and Being: The Plight of the Participant Observer in Emerson, James, Adams, and Faulkner* (Middletown, Conn.: Wesleyan University Press, 1981).

33. Sundquist, "The Country of the Blue," p. 7.

34. Ralph Ellison, "Change the Joke and Slip the Yoke," *Shadow and Act* (New York: Random House, 1964), p. 54.

35. Baker, *Blues, Ideology, and Afro-American Fiction: A Vernacular Study* (Chicago: University of Chicago Press, 1984), p. 200.

36. Toni Morrison, "Unspeakable Things Unspoken: The Afro-American Presence in American Literature," *Michigan Quarterly Review* 28.1 (1989): 11. See also Morrison, *Playing in the Dark: Whiteness and the Literary Imagination* (Cambridge, Mass.: Harvard University Press, 1992).

37. William Boelhower, *Through a Glass Darkly: Ethnic Semiosis in American Literature* (Venice: Edizioni Helvetia, 1984), p. 109.

38. Daniel J. Schneider, *The Crystal Cage: Adventures of the Imagination in the Fiction of Henry James* (Lawrence: Regents Press of Kansas, 1978), p. 7.

39. John David Smith, *An Old Creed for the New South: Proslavery Ideology and Historiography, 1865–1918* (Westport, Conn.: Greenwood Press, 1985), p. 4.

40. W. E. B. Du Bois, *The Souls of Black Folk*, in *Writings* (New York: Li-

brary of America, 1986), p. 364; Henry James, *The Ambassadors* (New York: Oxford University Press, 1964), p. 18; emphasis added.

41. See Arnold Rampersad, *The Art and Imagination of W. E. B. Du Bois* (Cambridge, Mass.: Harvard University Press, 1976), p. 74, for some of the possible sources for Du Bois's use of the term; the most comprehensive study of the relation of Du Bois's thinking to that of his contemporaries is Adolph Reed's forthcoming book on Du Bois.

42. Richard Slotkin, *Fatal Environment: The Idea of the Frontier in the Age of Industrialization, 1800–1890* (New York: Atheneum, 1985), p. 296.

43. Ernesto Laclau and Chantal Mouffe, *Hegemony and Socialist Strategy: Towards a Radical Democratic Politics* (London: Verso, 1985), p. 176.

44. R. W. B. Lewis, *The Jameses: A Family Narrative* (New York: Farrar, Straus and Giroux, 1991), p. 157.

45. Elaine Showalter, "A Criticism of Our Own," in *The Future of Literary Theory*, ed. Ralph Cohen (New York: Routledge, 1989), p. 358. The work to which Showalter refers is *"Race," Writing, and Difference*, ed. Gates (Chicago: University of Chicago Press, 1986).

46. Hazel V. Carby, *Reconstructing Womanhood: The Emergence of the Afro-American Woman Novelist* (New York: Oxford University Press, 1987), p. 18.

47. Theodore O. Mason, Jr., "Between the Populist and the Scientist: Ideology and Power in Recent Afro-American Literary Criticism; or, 'The Dozens' as Scholarship," *Callaloo* 11 (Summer 1988): 613.

48. See for example Kwame Anthony Appiah, "The Conservation of 'Race,'" *Black American Literature Forum* 23 (1989): 37–60; Carby, "The Canon: Civil War and Reconstruction," *Michigan Quarterly Review* 23 (1989): 35–43; Adolph Reed, Jr., "The 'Black Revolution' and the Reconstitution of Domination," in *Race, Politics, and Culture: Critical Essays on the Radicalism of the 1960s*, ed. Reed, (New York: Greenwood Press, 1986), pp. 61–95; and Werner Sollors, *Beyond Ethnicity: Consent and Descent in American Culture* (New York: Oxford University Press, 1986), and "A Critique of Pure Pluralism," *Reconstructing American Literary History* ed. Sacvan Bercovitch (Cambridge, Mass.: Harvard University Press, 1986), pp. 250–279;

49. Aldon Lynn Nielsen, *Reading Race: White American Poets and Racial Discourse in the Twentieth Century* (Athens: University of Georgia Press, 1988), p. 2.

50. See for example Michael Awkward, "Negotiations of Power: White Critics, Black Texts, and the Self-Referential Impulse," *American Literary History* 2 (1990): 593.

CHAPTER ONE

1. Besides the works by Borus, Seltzer, and Porter already cited, relevant studies on James include Jean-Christophe Agnew, "The Consuming

Vision of Henry James," in *The Culture of Consumption: Critical Essays in American History, 1880–1980*, ed. Richard Wrightman Fox and T. J. Jackson Lears (New York: Pantheon, 1983); Michael Anseko, *"Friction with the Market": Henry James and the Profession of Authorship* (New York: Oxford University Press, 1986); Marcia Jacobson, *Henry James and the Mass Market* (University: University of Alabama Press, 1983); and Jennifer Wicke, *Advertising Fictions: Literature, Advertisement, and Social Reading* (New York: Columbia University Press, 1988).

2. Henry James, "The Art of Fiction," in *The Art of Fiction and Other Essays* (New York: Oxford University Press, 1948), p. 384; subsequent citations to this essay will appear in the body of the text.

3. George M. Fredrickson, *The Inner Civil War: Northern Intellectuals and the Crisis of the Union* (New York: Harper and Row, 1965), p. 165. Upon seeing a model of the monument to Colonel Robert Shaw, Ralph Ellison observed "that since I was writing fiction and seeking vaguely for images of black and white fraternity I would do well to recall that Henry James's brother Wilky had fought as an officer with those Negro soldiers, and that Colonel Shaw's body had been thrown into a ditch with those of his men." (Ellison, introduction to *Invisible Man* [1952; New York: Vintage 1990], p. xvii).

4. James, *Notes of a Son and Brother*, in *Autobiography*, ed. Frederick W. Dupee (New York: Criterion Books, 1956), p. 457.

5. James, *A Small Boy and Others*, in *Autobiography*, p. 143.

6. James, *The Portrait of a Lady*, ed. Robert D. Bamberg (New York: W. W. Norton, 1975) p. 60; *The Wings of the Dove*, ed. J. Donald Crowley and Richard Hocks (New York: W. W. Norton, 1978), p. 231.

7. James, *The American Scene* (Bloomington: Indiana University Press, 1968), p. 375.

8. Maxwell Geismar, *Henry James and the Jacobites* (Boston: Houghton Mifflin, 1963), p. 154.

9. Henry James, "Democracy and Theodore Roosevelt." *The American Essays of Henry James*, ed. Leon Edel (New York: Vintage, 1956), p. 215.

10. Boelhower, *Through a Glass Darkly*, p. 21.

11. James, *The American Scene*, p. 139.

12. See John Higham, *Strangers in the Land: Patterns of American Nativism 1860–1925* (New York: Atheneum, 1981), pp. 141–49.

13. James, *The American Scene*, p. 375.

14. Carl S. Smith, "James's International Fiction: Sources and Evolution," *The Centennial Review* 23 (1979): 399.

15. Howells, *An Imperative Duty*, vol. 17 of *A Selected Edition of William Dean Howells*, ed. Robert Gottesman (Bloomington: Indiana University Press, 1970), p. 6.

16. Higham, *Strangers in the Land,* p. 20.
17. Bishop T. U. Dudley, "How Shall We Help the Negro," *Century,* 30 (June 1885), p. 274.
18. James, preface to *The Portrait of A Lady,* ed. Robert D. Bamberg (New York: W. W. Norton, 1975), p. 13.
19. James, "Criticism," in *The Art of Fiction and Other Essays,* p. 215.
20. James, preface to *The Ambassadors,* p. 3.
21. Philip Fisher, *Hard Facts: Setting and Form in the American Novel* (New York: Oxford University Press, 1985), p. 99.
22. Alexis de Tocqueville, *Democracy in America,* 2 vols. (New York: Vintage Books, 1945), 2:345.
23. William James, "The Philippine Question" (1899), *The Works of William James: Essays, Comments, and Reviews,* ed. Frederick H. Burkhardt et al. (Cambridge, Mass.: Harvard University Press, 1987), p. 160.
24. Du Bois, *The Souls of Black Folk,* p. 462.
25. James, *The Princess Casamassima,* ed. Derek Brewer (New York: Penguin, 1987), p. 164.
26. James, preface to *The Wings of the Dove,* ed. J. Donald Crowley and Richard Hocks (New York: W. W. Norton, 1978), p. 6.
27. See Charles Feidelson, "The Moment of *The Portrait of a Lady*," *Ventures* 8 (1968): 47–55.
28. James, preface to *The Princess Casamassima,* pp. 35, 39.
29. Ibid., pp. 36, 38, 36.
30. James, preface to *The Portrait of a Lady,* pp. 9–10; subsequent citations to this volume will appear in the body of the text.
31. James, *The Complete Notebooks of Henry James,* ed. Leon Edel and Lyall H. Powers (New York: Oxford University Press, 1987), pp. 55, 6.
32. Edel, *Henry James: The Middle Years, 1882–1895* (Philadelphia: Lippincott, 1962), p. 47.
33. James, *The Complete Notebooks of Henry James,* p. 13.
34. James, "The Point of View," *The Novels and Tales of Henry James,* vol. 14 of the New York Edition (1908; New York: Charles Scribner's and Sons, 1936), pp. 603, 592; subsequent citations to this story will appear in the body of the text.
35. James, "Criticism," p. 217.
36. Seltzer, *Henry James and the Art of Power,* pp. 147, 148, 126.
37. Higham, *Strangers in the Land,* p. 36.
38. Quoted in Chalres A. Lofgren, *The Plessy Case: A Legal-Historical Interpretation* (New York: Oxford University Press, 1987), p. 71.
39. James, preface to vol. 14 of the New York Edition, p. xxi.
40. See Edel, *Henry James: The Middle Years,* pp. 49–50.
41. Cable, "The Silent South," in *The Negro Question,* pp. 87, 88, 83.
42. James, *The American Scene,* p. 375.

43. "The Era of Sociology," *American Journal of Sociology* 1 (July 1895): 1, 2.

44. See Higham, *Strangers in the Land*, pp. 12–34.

45. Slotkin, *Fatal Environment*, p. 282.

46. Quoted in Lofgren, *The Plessy Case*, p. 166.

47. Lofgren, *The Plessy Case*, pp. 114–15. My account of the legal environment surrounding race legislation is heavily indebted to Lofgren's study of this period. The other accounts of race relations during this period that have been crucial to my work are Fredrickson, *The Black Image in the White Mind: The Debate of Afro-American Character and Destiny, 1817–1914* (New York: Harper and Row, 1971) and Joel A. Williamson, *The Crucible of Race: Black-White Relations in the American South since Emancipation* (New York: Oxford University Press, 1984).

48. James, "Criticism," p. 217.

49. C. Vann Woodward, *The Strange Career of Jim Crow*, rev. ed., (New York: Oxford University Press, 1966), p. 97.

50. Lofgren, *The Plessy Case*, pp. 91, 53.

51. Cable, "The Silent South," p. 83.

52. James, "American Democracy and American Education," in *The American Essays of Henry James*, p. 243.

53. Erich Auerbach, *Mimesis: The Representation of Reality in Western Literature* (Princeton: Princeton University Press, 1953), p. 552.

54. Howells, "Editor's Study" (Apr. 1886), in *Editor's Study*, p. 22. Amy Kaplan notes that Howells "anticipates Erich Auerbach's well-known definition of nineteenth-century realism as the breakdown of neoclassical styles." She also suggests that "for Howells, the democratization of literary representation was less the triumphant revolution that Auerbach suggests than a contradictory struggle to form bonds between members of antagonistic social classes" (*The Social Construction of American Realism*, p. 22).

55. Irving Howe, *Politics and the Novel* (New York: Fawcett, 1967), pp. 166–67.

56. Cable, "The Silent South," p. 81.

57. See Leon F. Litwack, *Been in the Storm So Long: The Aftermath of Slavery* (New York: Vintage Books, 1979), pp. 261–91.

58. Cable, "The Freedman's Case in Equity," in *The Negro Question*, pp. 53, 67.

59. James, preface to *The Princess Casamassima*, p. 39.

60. See Lofgren, *The Plessy Case*, pp. 93–115.

61. *Giles v. Harris* (189 U.S. 475). I am indebted to Brook Thomas for bringing this case to my attention.

62. See Seltzer, *Henry James and the Art of Power*, pp. 48–58.

63. James, *The Princess Casamassima*, pp. 491, 487; subsequent citations to this novel will appear in the body of the text.

64. "A New Volume of 'The Century,'" *Century,* July 1885, p. 164.

65. Ibid., pp. 164–165.

66. Dudley, "How Shall We Help the Negro," p. 274.

67. Cable, "The Silent South," p. 83.

CHAPTER TWO

1. Roswell Smith, letter to Howells, 17 Mar. 1885, rpt. *The Rise of Silas Lapham,* ed. Don L. Cook (1885; New York: W. W. Norton, 1982), p. 377.

2. Henry James, *The Princess Casamassima,* p. 478.

3. Howells, *Editor's Study,* p. 169.

4. Thomas Sergeant Perry, "William Dean Howells," *Century* 23 (Mar., 1882), pp. 684, 683.

5. Cable, "The Due Restraints and Liberties of Literature," in *The Negro Question,* p. 48.

6. C. Vann Woodward, *The Strange Career of Jim Crow.* Also see Alan Pendleton Grimes, *The Political Liberalism of the New York "Nation," 1865–1932* (Chapel Hill: University of North Carlina Press, 1953, esp. pp. 11, 18–19, and Slotkin's *Fatal Environment,* pp. 490–494 on the changing politics of Northern magazines and periodicals.

7. Perry, "William Dean Howells," p. 685.

8. Cable, "The Silent South," in *The Negro Question,* p. 83.

9. "Topics of the Time," *Century,* 24 (1882) p. 940.

10. R. W. Gilder, letter to W. C. P Breckinridge, 24 June 1885, in *Letters of Richard Watson Gilder,* ed. Rosamond Gilder (New York: Houghton Mifflin Co., 1916), pp. 130–31.

11. Gilder, letter to Edmund Gosse, 2 Nov. 1885, *Letters,* p. 176.

12. "The Essence of the Reconstruction Question," *The Nation,* 1 (6 July 1865), p. 4.

13. See Michael Les Benedict, "Reform Republicans and the Retreat from Reconstruction," in *The Facts of Reconstruction: Essays in Honor of John Hope Franklin,* ed. Eric Anderson and Alfred A. Moss, Jr. (Baton Rouge: Louisiana State University Press, 1991), pp. 64–71.

14. Gilder, letter to Mark Twain, January 8, 1886, *Letters,* pp. 398, 399. In this letter Gilder quotes to Twain portions of a response he had given to a subscriber who had complained about the *Century's* publication of Twain's works.

15. Gilder, letter to George Washington Cable, 1 Feb. 1882, *Letters,* p. 390.

16. Quoted in Arlin W. Turner, *George Washington Cable, A Biography,* (Durham, N.C.: Duke University Press, 1956), p. 29.

17. Albion W. Tourgée, *A Fool's Errand* (Cambridge: Harvard University Press, 1961), pp. 387, 171, 378.

18. Quoted in Herbert F. Smith, *Richard Watson Gilder* (New York: Twayne, 1970), p. 71.

19. Quoted in Carby, *Reconstructing Womanhood*, p. 86. Booker T. Washington's famed "Atlanta Exposition Address" offered whites similar assurances, reminding Southerners that blacks, unlike foreigners, had "without strikes and labour wars, tilled your fields, cleared your forests" (Booker T. Washington, *Up From Slavery*, in *Three Negro Classics* [New York: Avon, 1965], p. 147).

20. Quoted in Kenneth S. Lynn, *William Dean Howells, An American Life* (New York: Harcourt Brace Jovanovich, Inc., 1971), p. 280.

21. See Carby, *Reconstructing Womanhood*, pp. 67–68 on this point.

22. Cable, "The Silent South," p. 118.

23. Cable, "The Freedman's Case in Equity," p. 63.

24. Howells, *Editor's Study*, p. 81.

25. Howells, letter to Henry James, 25 Dec. 1886, in *Selected Letters*, ed. Robert C. Leitz III, vol. 3 of *A Selected Edition of William Dean Howells*, p. 174.

26. Howells, *Editor's Study*, pp. 328, 199.

27. Ibid., p. 200.

28. Howells, "Equality as the Basis of Good Society," *Century*, 51 (Nov. 1895), p. 63.

29. Howells, *Silas Lapham*, pp. 171–72.

30. Quoted in Lynn, *William Dean Howells*, p. 280.

31. Howells, *Silas Lapham*, p. 172.

32. See "Textual Variations: The Dynamite Passage," in *Silas Lapham*, pp. 341–42.

33. Quoted in Lynn, *William Dean Howells*, p. 280.

34. Edwin Cady, *The Realist at War*, (Syracuse, N.Y.: Syracuse University Press, 1958), p. 289.

35. Letter to the editor of the *New York Tribune*, 12 Nov. 1887, in *Selected Letters*, p. 204.

36. Roswell Smith, letter to Howells, 18 Feb. 1885, in *Silas Lapham*, p. 340.

37. Quoted in Cady, *The Realist at War*, p. 90.

38. Julia Ward Howe, *Is Polite Society Polite? and Other Essays* (Boston: Houghton, Mifflin and Co., 1899), p. 23.

39. Howells, *Silas Lapham*, p. 190.

40. Howells, *Editor's Study*, p. 41.

41. Howells, *A Modern Instance* (New York: Penguin Books, 1977), p. 265.

42. Ida B. Wells, *Southern Horrors: Lynch Law in All Its Phases*, in *Selected Works of Ida B. Wells-Barnett*, comp. Trudier Harris (1892; New York: Oxford University Press, 1991), p. 31.

43. William James, "Epidemic of Lynching," *Boston Journal,* 29 July 1903, p. 1; rpt. in James, *Essays, Comments, and Reviews* (Cambridge, Mass.: Harvard University Press, 1987), pp. 173–74.

44. Howells, *The Minister's Charge; or, The Apprenticeship of Lemuel Barker,* vol. 14 of *A Selected Edition of W. D. Howells,* p. 341.

45. Quoted in Lynn, *William Dean Howells,* p. 296.

46. Howells, *Annie Kilburn* (New York: Harper & Brothers, 1889), p. 325.

47. Howells, *An Imperative Duty,* p. 93.

48. Du Bois, "Howells and Black Folk," *Writings,* p. 1147.

49. Claudia Tate, "Allegories of Black Female Desire; or, Rereading Nineteenth-Century Sentimental Narratives of Black Female Authority," in *Changing Our Own Words: Essays on Criticism, Theory, and Writing by Black Women,* ed. Cheryl A. Wall (New Brunswick, N.J.: Rutgers University Press, 1989), p. 101.

50. Baker, *Workings of the Spirit: The Poetics of Afro-American Women's Writing* (Chicago: University of Chicago Press, 1991), p. 34.

51. Frances E. W. Harper, *Iola Leroy, or Shadows Uplifted,* (New York: Oxford University Press, 1988), p. 235, 89.

52. Ibid., p. 263.

53. Carby, *Reconstructing Womanhood,* p. 93.

54. Anna Julia Cooper, *A Voice from the South* (1892; New York: Oxford University Press, 1988), pp. 201, 206.

55. Howells, *An Imperative Duty,* p. 5.

56. Cooper, *A Voice from the South,* pp. 206–7.

57. Latimer says: "To-day, . . . the negro is not plotting in beer-saloons against the peace and order of society. His fingers are not dripping with dynamite, neither is he spitting upon your flag, nor flaunting the red banner of anarchy in your face" (Harper, *Iola Leroy,* p. 223).

58. Cooper, *A Voice from the South,* pp. 173, 255, 139.

59. The rise of these alliances created some tension between black Republicans and black agrarians: "In Virginia, North Carolina, South Carolina, Alabama, and Texas, entrenched black Republican leaders systematically undercut the efforts of organizers for the Negro Alliance. . . . The agrarian revolt thus divided both races, whites along economic lines and blacks according to decisions based on cold and necessary calculations of political and physical survival" (Lawrence Goodwyn, *The Populist Moment: A Short History of the Agrarian Revolt in America* [New York: Oxford University Press, 1978], pp. 121–22).

60. Cooper, *A Voice from the South,* p. 255.

CHAPTER THREE

1. William Veeder, *Henry James—The Lesson of the Master: Popular Fiction and Personal Style in the Nineteenth Century* (Chicago: University of Chi-

cago Press, 1978), p. 7. More recently *New Essays on Uncle Tom's Cabin* ed. Sundquist (New York: Cambridge University Press, 1986) further investigates the continuing influence of Stowe on American letters. See especially Richard Yarborough, "Strategies of Black Characterization in *Uncle Tom's Cabin* and the Early Afro-American Novel," pp. 45–84.

2. John William De Forest, "The Great American Novel," *The Nation* 6 (9 Jan. 1868), p. 27; Howells, *My Literary Passions* (1891; New York: Harper & Brothers, 1895), p. 50. Later, in a speech published in the *North American Review* (Apr. 1912), Howells called *Uncle Tom's Cabin* "that most essentially American novel" (rpt. as "Mr. Howells's Speech" in *Criticism and Fiction and Other Essays*, ed. Clara Marburg Kirk and Rudolf Kirk (New York: New York University Press, 1959), pp. 366–74).

3. Quoted in John Hope Franklin, introduction to *A Fool's Errand*, p. xx.

4. George L. Aiken, "Uncle Tom's Cabin," *Dramas from the American Theatre, 1762–1909*, ed. Richard Moody (Cleveland: World Publishing Co., 1966), p. 349.

5. James, *A Small Boy and Others*, p. 95.

6. See Raymond A. Cook, *Thomas Dixon* (New York: Twayne Publishers, 1974), p. 66, and Williams, *The Crucible of Race*, p. 157.

7. Cooper, *A Voice from the South*, pp. 180, 222.

8. Veeder, *The Lesson of the Master*, p. 15.

9. Alfred Kazin, "Grandeur and Misery of Realism," in *Impressions of a Gilded Age: The American Fin de Siècle*, ed. Marc Chenetier and Rob Kroes, European Contributions to American Studies 6 (Amsterdam: Amerika Instituut, University of Amsterdam, 1983), p. 133.

10. De Forest, "The Great American Novel," p. 27.

11. Fisher, *Hard Facts*, p. 126.

12. Charles Dickens, *Little Dorritt*, ed. Peter Sucksmith (New York: Oxford University Press, 1977), p. 70.

13. Yarborough provides an excellent summary of these charges against Stowe; see "Strategies of Black Characterization," pp. 45–50).

14. Francis A. Shoup, "*Uncle Tom's Cabin:* Forty Years After," in *Critical Essays on Harriet Beecher Stowe*, ed. Elizabeth Ammons (Boston: G. K. Hall, 1980), p. 50.

15. See Fredrickson, *The Black Image in the White Mind*, pp. 101–2 on Stowe's romantic racism.

16. René Wellek, "Realism in Literary Scholarship," in *Concepts of Criticism*, ed. Stephen G. Nichols, Jr. (New Haven, Conn.: Yale University Press, 1963), p. 226.

17. De Forest, *Miss Ravenel's Conversion from Secession to Loyalty*, p. 237, 236.

18. See Laurence Holland, "A Raft of Trouble," in *American Realism*,

pp. 75–78, and Everett Carter, "The Modernist Ordeal of Huckleberry Finn," *Studies in American Fiction* 13 (Autumn 1985): 170.

19. Howell, *Editor's Study*, p. 38.

20. Howells, "Equality as the Basis of Good Society," p. 63.

21. Ibid.

22. On the fear of savagery during this period see Slotkin, *Fatal Environment*, and Alan Trachtenberg, *The Incorporation of America: Culture and Society in the Gilded Age* (New York: Hill and Wang, 1982).

23. Howells, *Silas Lapham*, p. 103.

24. Howells, *Editor's Study*, p. 95.

25. Kaplan, *The Social Construction of American Realism*, p. 21.

26. Cable, "The Freedman's Case in Equity," p. 64.

27. Du Bois, *The Souls of Black Folk*, p. 477.

28. Charles W. Chesnutt, *The Marrow of Tradition* (Ann Arbor: University of Michigan Press, 1973), p. 61.

29. Woodward, *The Strange Career of Jim Crow*, p. 107.

30. Charles Sumner, "Clemency and Common Sense: A Curiousity of Literature with a Moral," *Atlantic Monthly* 17 (Dec. 1865), p. 759.

31. Howells, *Editor's Study*, p. 96.

32. Du Bois, "The Conservation of Races," in *Writings*, p. 825.

33. See Kaplan, *The Social Construction of American Realism*, pp. 21–25.

34. Howells, "Novel-Writing and Novel-Reading: An Impersonal Explanation," in *The Norton Anthology of American Literature*, 2d ed., ed. Nina Baym, et al., 2. vols. (New York: W. W. Norton, 1985), 2:293.

35. Howells, *Silas Lapham* pp. 112–13.

36. Ibid., p. 319.

37. June Howard who observes that in realistic novels "the depiction of profound social change, which would propel us from the present into utopian or science fiction, is generically proscribed. The choices that remain to the characters may be imbued with personal or metaphysical meaning, but they can never be adequate to the central social themes of the novel" (*Form and History in American Literary Naturalism*, p. 145).

38. Howells, *Silas Lapham*, p. 315.

39. Howells, "An East-Side Ramble," *Impressions and Experiences* (New York: Harper & Brothers, 1896), p. 110.

40. Frederick Douglass, *The Life and Times of Frederick Douglass* (New York: Collier Books, 1962), p. 438.

41. Du Bois, "The Conservation of Races," p. 824.

42. In assessing Du Bois's writings from the 1890s, Lofgren's *The Plessy Case* argues that "*taken selectively* his comments provided confirmation for the position that Negroes constituted a distinctive group, too often with debilitating characteristics and needing segregated institutions" (p. 114).

43. Cable, "The Silent South," p. 89.

44. Howell, *Silas Lapham*, p. 317.

45. Ibid., p. 314.

46. On blackness as a mark of the unassimilable, see James Kinney, *Amalgamation! Race, Sex, and Rhetoric in the Nineteenth-Century American Novel* (Westport, Conn.: Greenwood Press, 1985), pp. 151–81.

47. Cable, *The Grandissimes: A Story of Creole Life* (1880; New York: Charles Scribner's Sons, 1918), p. 331.

48. For more detailed discussions of the ways in which this view dovetailed with contemporary scientific and legalistic thinking, see Fredrickson, *The Black Image in the White Mind;* John S. Haller, Jr., *Outcasts from Evolution: Scientific Attitudes of Racial Inferiority, 1859–1900* (Urbana: University of Illinois Press, 1971); and Lofgren, *The Plessy Case.*

49. Cable, *Miss Ravenel's Conversion*, pp. 220, 448.

50. Ibid., pp. 219–20.

51. Ibid., p. 448.

52. Ibid., pp. 51, 10.

53. Ibid., pp. 4, 3, 50.

54. Ibid., p. 219.

55. Ibid., p. 48.

56. Harper, *Iola Leroy*, p. 217.

57. Gilder, letter to W. C. P. Breckinridge, 24 June 1885, in *Letters*, p. 131.

58. Quoted in Lofgren, *The Plessy Case*, p. 145.

59. Dunning, *Essays on the Civil War and Reconstruction and Related Topics* (1897; New York: Peter Smith, 1931), pp. 251, 384.

60. Madison Grant, *The Passing of the Great Race, or the Racial Basis of European History* (New York: Charles Scribner's Sons, 1916), p. 14.

61. Fisher, *Hard Facts*, pp. 92, 99, 93.

62. Howells, "Criticism and Fiction," p. 15.

63. Fiedler, *The Inadvertent Epic: From "Uncle Tom's Cabin" to "Roots"* (New York: Simon and Schuster, 1979), p. 26.

64. William R. Taylor, *Cavalier and Yankee: The Old South and American National Character* (Garden City, N.Y.: Doubleday, 1963), p. 26.

65. Harriet Beecher Stowe, *Uncle Tom's Cabin; or, Life Among the Lowly* (1852; New York: Harper and Row, 1965), p. 160.

66. DeForest, *Miss Ravenel's Conversion from Secession to Loyalty*, p. 19; Henry James, *The Bostonians*, p. 10; Howells, *An Imperative Duty*, p. 24; Thomas Dixon, Jr., *The Leopard's Spots: A Romance of the White Man's Burden* (New York: Doubleday, Page and Co., 1903), p. 45.

67. James, *The Bostonians*, p. 87; subsequent citations to this novel will appear in the body of the text.

68. Quoted in Wilson, *Patriotic Gore*, p. 3.

69. Wicke, *Advertising Fictions*, p. 99.

70. Ibid., p. 100.

71. James, "The New Novel," in *The Art of Fiction and Other Essays*, pp. 210, 187, 187.

72. Judith Fetterly, in *The Resisting Reader: A Feminist Approach to American Fiction* (Bloomington: Indiana University Press, 1978), also notices crucial similarities between Miss Birdseye and Dr. Prance, but she sees Olive as differing from these two: "Indeed, the ultimate similarity between Miss Birdseye and Dr. Prance . . . is the degree to which each has given up her sexuality in order to accomplish her goals. Olive's potential effectuality can be measured by the fact that she is not so willing to do so" (p. 141).

73. James, *A Small Boy and Others*, p. 95.

74. Ibid., p. 93.

75. Charles Dudley Warner, "The Story of *Uncle Tom's Cabin,*" in *Critical Essays on Harriet Beecher Stowe*, p. 67. See also Aiken, "Uncle Tom's Cabin," pp. 349–50.

76. Shoup, *"Uncle Tom's Cabin,"* p. 50.

77. Quoted in Thomas P. Riggio, *"Uncle Tom* Reconstructed: A Neglected Chapter in the History of a Book," in *Critical Essays on Harriet Beecher Stowe*, p. 142. Riggio provides a perceptive reading of the relationship between Stowe and Southern racist writers, arguing that more than the "Tom Shows" the work of Dixon, Thomas Nelson Page, and others contributed to the transformation of Uncle Tom from a symbol of black hope to a symbol of black repression.

78. James, "The Art of Fiction," p. 21.

79. See for example Geismar, *Henry James and the Jacobites*, p. 64; Clinton Oliver, "Henry James as a Social Critic," *Antioch Review* 7 (1947): 243–58; and Lionel Trilling, *"The Bostonians,"* in *The Opposing Self* (New York: Viking, 1955), pp. 100–103.

80. Dixon, *The Leopard's Spots*, p. 45; subsequent citations to this novel will appear in the body of the text. Though Riggio fails to take up the issue of sentimentalism as a genre and does not expand his question of Stowe's influence beyond Southern writers, my reading of *The Leopard's Spots* against *Uncle Tom' Cabin* is indebted to Riggio's study. See note 77 above.

81. Howells, *An Imperative Duty*, p. 24.

82. Tourgée, *A Fool's Errand*, p. 119.

83. Quoted in Carby, *Reconstructing Womanhood*, p. 130.

84. Du Bois, *The Souls of Black Folk*, p. 380.

85. James, *A Small Boy and Others*, p. 95.

86. James, preface to *The Ambassadors* (New York: Oxford University Press, 1964), p. 4.

87. Dixon, preface to *The Leopard's Spots*, n.p.

88. Cook, *Thomas Dixon*, p. 65.

89. See Cady, *The Realist at War*, pp. 208–9.

90. James, "Criticism," pp. 217, 215, 215.
91. Ibid., p. 217.
92. James, preface to *The Portrait of a Lady*, p. 13.
93. Quoted in *The Thin Disguise: Turning Point in Negro History, Plessy v. Ferguson, A Documentary Presentation (1864–1896)*, ed. Otto H. Olsen (New York: Humanities Press, 1967), p. 111.
94. Ziff, *The American 1890s*, p. 227.
95. Dunning, *Essays on the Civil War and Reconstruction*, p. 384.

CHAPTER FOUR

1. James, *The American Scene*, pp. 465, 406; hereafter abbreviated *A*.
2. Harper, *Iola Leroy*, p. 219; hereafter abbreviated *I*.
3. Tourgée, quoted in *The Thin Disguise*, p. 83.
4. I am indebted to Mark Goble for pointing out the employment of the Faust myth in tales of "passing" like James Weldon Johnson's *Autobiography of an Ex-Colored Man*.
5. William James, letter to Henry James, 6 June 1903, *Letters of William James*, ed. Henry James, 2 vols. (Boston: Atlantic Monthly Press, 1920) 2: 196.
6. Du Bois, *The Souls of Black Folk*, p. 547; hereafter abbreviated *S*.
7. Porter, *Seeing and Being*, p. 133.
8. Robert Stepto, *From Behind the Veil: A Study of Afro-American Narrative* (Urbana: University of Illinois Press, 1979), p. 59. See also pp. 82–91 for further charting of Du Bois's revisions of Washington.
9. Washington, *Up From Slavery*, p. 76.
10. Du Bois, *Writings*, p. 1286.
11. Du Bois, *Dusk of Dawn*, in *Writings*, p. 573.
12. See Kenneth W. Warren, "Possessing the Common Ground: William Dean Howells's *An Imperative Duty*," *American Literary Realism, 1870–1910* 20 (1988): 27.
13. Howells, *An Imperative Duty*, p. 7.
14. Berndt Ostendorf, *Black Literature in White America* (New York: Barnes and Noble Press., 1982), p. 78.
15. James, *A Small Boy and Others*, p. 142.
16. See Stepto, *From Behind the Veil*, p. 78–79, on Du Bois's criticism of the plantation school.
17. Donna Przybylowicz, *Desire and Repression: The Dialectic of Self and Other in the Late Works of Henry James* (University: University of Alabama Press, 1986), p. 266.
18. See James, *Notes of a Son and Brother*, esp. pp. 274–300.
19. Henry James, "The Jolly Corner," *The Novels and Tales of Henry James*, vol. 17 of the New York Edition (1909), pp. 435, 448, 438; hereafter abbreviated *J*.

20. Leon Edel, "Henry James: The Dramatic Years," in *The Complete Plays of Henry James* (Philadelphia: Lippincott, 1949), p. 23.

21. Carl Wittke, *Tambo and Bones: A History of the American Minstrel Stage* (Westport, Conn.: Greenwood Press, 1968), p. 37. On the ubiquity of minstrel performances on the American stage, see also George C. D. Odell, vol. 4 of *Annals of the New York Stage* (New York: Columbia University Press, 1931).

22. See Harry Reynolds, *Minstrel Memories: The Story of Burnt Cork Minstrelsy in Great Britain from 1836 to 1937* (London: Alston Rivers, Ltd., 1928), pp. 77–78. On the Christmas tradition of minstrelsy, see the excerpt from the diary entry of Charles DeLong in Alexander Saxton, *The Rise and Fall of the White Republic: Class Politics and Mass Culture in Nineteenth-Century America* (New York: Verso, 1990), p. 172. Also particularly helpful here is Gates's discussion of black harlequin in *Figures in Black*, pp. 51–53.

23. James, *A Small Boy and Others*, pp. 181, 98.

24. Ibid., p. 302.

25. Saxton, *The Rise and Fall of the White Republic*, p. 168.

26. Edel, "The Dramatic Years," pp. 51, 52, 52, 51.

27. Lawrence W. Levine, *Highbrow/Lowbrow: The Emergence of Cultural Hierarchy in America* (Cambridge, Mass.: Harvard University Press, 1988), p. 177.

CONCLUSION

1. Joyce A. Joyce, "The Black Canon: Reconstructing Black American Literary Criticism," *New Literary History* 18 (1986): 343.

2. See Baker, "In Dubious Battle," *New Literary History* 18 (1987): 363–69; Gates, "'What's Love Got to Do With It?': Critical Theory, Integrity, and the Black Idiom," *New Literary History* 18 (1987): 345–62; and Joyce's rejoinder in that same issue, "'Who the Cap Fit': Unconscionableness in the Criticism of Houston A. Baker, Jr., and Henry Louis Gates, Jr.": 371–84.

3. The critical assessments of this debate have proliferated. See for example, Appiah, "The Conservation of 'Race'"; Awkward, "Race, Gender, and the Politics of Reading," *Black American Literature Forum* 22 (Spring 1988); Diana Fuss, *Essentially Speaking: Feminism, Nature, and Difference* (New York: Routledge, 1987), pp. 73–96; Mason, Valerie Smith, "Black Feminist Theory and the Representation of the 'Other,'" in *Changing Our Own Words: Essays on Criticism, Theory, and Writing by Black Women*, ed. Cheryl A. Wall (New Brunswick, N.J.: Rutgers University Press, 1989), pp. 38–57.

4. Baker, *Workings of the Spirit*, pp. 32, 30.

5. Mason, "Between the Populist and the Scientist," p. 608.

6. Baker, *Workings of the Spirit*, p. 30.

7. Ibid., pp. 30, 205, 31.

8. Ibid., p. 19.

9. Fuss, *Essentially Speaking*, pp. 94–95. bell hooks dissents profoundly from Fuss's and Baker's observations; see her "Essentialism and Experience," *American Literary History* 3 (1991): 172–83.

10. See also Mason, "Between the Populist and the Scientist," p. 609.

11. Baker, *Workings of the Spirit*, p. 18; Gates, *Figures in Black*, p. 54; Awkward, "Response," in *Afro-American Literary Study in the 1990s*, p. 77.

12. Awkward; "Race, Gender, and the Politics of Reading," p. 6.

13. Carby, "The Canon: Civil War and Reconstruction," p. 42.

14. Awkward, "Race, Gender, and the Politics of Reading," p. 24.

15. Mason, "Between the Populist and the Scientist," pp. 607–8.

16. Gates, *Figures in Black*, p. 56.

17. Awkward, *Inspiriting Influences: Tradition, Revision, and Afro-American Women's Novels* (New York: Columbia University Press, 1989), p. 9.

18. Jameson, *The Political Unconscious*, p. 152.

19. Awkward, "Response," p. 77.

20. Reed, "The 'Black Revolution' and the Reconstitution of Domination," p. 76.

21. Baker, *Blues, Ideology, and Afro-American Fiction*, p. 196.

22. Ibid., pp. 200, 195, 196, 195.

23. Michaels, *The Gold Standard and the Logic of Naturalism*, p. 27.

24. For an extended critique of Michaels's position, see Jameson, *Postmodernism or, The Cultural Logic of Late Capitalism* (Durham, N.C.: Duke University Press, 1991), pp. 181–217.

25. Reed, "The 'Black Revolution,'" pp. 78–79, 76.

26. Baker, *Blues, Ideology, and Afro-American Fiction*, p.197.

27. Reed, "The 'Black Revolution,'" p. 82.

28. See Carby, "The Canon," p. 42; Reed, "The 'Black Revolution,'" p. 75; Warren, "Delimiting America: The Legacy of Du Bois," *American Literary History* 1 (Spring 1989) p. 187.

29. Morrison, "Unspeakable Things Unspoken," p. 11.

30. Representative here is Houston Baker's remark that "even as I recall a pleasurable spring in New Haven when I enjoyed cracking Joycean codes in order to teach *Ulysses*, I realise that the Irish writer's grand monument is not a work to which I shall return with reverence. . . . I am certain that I shall never place *Ulysses* in a group of texts that I describe, to use Trilling's words, as "spiritual" if not "actually religious" (Baker, *Modernism and the Harlem Renaissance,* [Chicago: University of Chicago Press, 1987], p. 7).

31. On the value of contingency, see Reed, "The 'Black Revolution,'" p. 83.

32. Gates, *The Signifying Monkey*, p. xxiii.

33. Gates, *Figures in Black*, p. xxii. See also Mason, "Between the Populist and the Scientist," p. 609.

34. William J. Bennett, *To Reclaim a Legacy: A Report on the Humanities in Higher Education* (Washington, D.C.: National Endowment for the Humanities, 1984), p. 9.

35. James Joyce, "Araby," *Dubliners* (Middlesex: Penguin Books, 1967), pp. 31, 35.

36. Bennett, *To Reclaim a Legacy*, p. 30.

37. See Laclau and Mouffe, *Hegemony and Socialist Strategy*, pp. 171–75.

INDEX

Abolitionism, 91; and Henry James, 19; in *The Bostonians*, 97; in antebellum fiction, 25; discrediting of, 108; and tradition of New England reform, 103, 104
Adventures of Huckleberry Finn, The (Twain), 1, 8, 53, 76
Ambassadors, The (James), 12, 103–5
American 1890s, The (Ziff), 2
American Journal of Sociology, 39
American Negro Academy, 80, 83
American Scene, The (James), 12, 15, 20–22, 34, 39, 111–16, 120–24, 139–40
Annie Kilburn (Howells), 61, 64, 68, 80
Anthony, Susan B., 55
Appiah, Kwame Anthony, 16
April Hopes (Howells), 64
"Araby" (Joyce), 142
"Art of Fiction, The" (James), 18, 24, 26, 101
Atlanta Cotton Exposition, 110, 117
Atlantic Monthly, 12, 20, 51, 79, 83
Auerbach, Erich, 41–42
Aunt Sylvia (escaped slave), 19, 120
Autobiography (James), 126
Awkward, Michael, 135–36

Baker, Houston A., 131–40
Bakhtinian dialogism, 136
Baldwin, James, 132
Barnum, P. T., 126
Barnum's Great American Museum, 126

Barnum's Lecture Hall, 126
"Battle Hymn of the Republic, The" (Howe, Julia), 61
Beloved (Morrison), 7
Bennett, William, 143
Bersani, Leo, 2–3, 8–10
Besant, Walter, 24
Blues, Ideology, and Afro-American Fiction (Baker), 140
Blues criticism. *See* Vernacular criticism
Boelhower, William, 11, 21
Bone, Robert, 4
Bostonian, The (James), 5, 93–101
Bradley, Justice Joseph, 107
Bricks without Straw (Tourgee), 103
Broadway Theatre, 126
Brown, John, 60
Brown, Sterling, 4
Burton's Theatre, 126

Cable, George Washington, 1–2, 13, 38–39, 42–43, 46–47, 50–56, 61, 67, 69, 72, 78, 83–85, 107. Works: *Dr. Sevier*, 53; "The Freedman's Case in Equity," 42–43, 47, 50–51, 55; *The Grandissimes*, 85; *John March, Southerner*, 54–55; "My Politics," 2; "The Silent South," 55–56
Capitalism, 9; and black emancipation, 119; consumer or market capitalism, 15, 18, 137, 138
Carby, Hazel, 16, 135–36
Century, 14, 20, 23, 38, 42, 46–56, 49, 61, 63, 71, 90, 93